SEEKING WITH ALL MY HEART

OTHER BOOKS BY PAULA D'ARCY

A New Set of Eyes
((The Crossroad Publishing Co., 2002)

Red Fire / A Quest for Awakening
(Innesfree Press, Inc., 2001)

Gift of the Red Bird / A Spiritual Encounter
(The Crossroad Publishing Co., 1996)

When Your Friend Is Grieving / Building a Bridge of Love
(Harold Shaw Publishers, 1990)

Where the Wind Begins / Stories of Hurting People
Who Said Yes to Life
(Harold Shaw Publishers, 1984)

Song for Sarah / A Mother's Journey through Grief and Beyond
(Harold Shaw Publishers, 1979; Waterbrook Press, 2001)

The Crossroad Publishing Company
www.CrossroadPublishing.com

Scripture quotations are taken from the following versions:
The Holy Bible, New International Version, copyright 1973, 1978, 1984 by the International Bible Society. Used by permission of Zondervan Bible Publishers.
The New Revised Standard Version Bible, copyright 1989 by the Division of Christian Education of the National Council of the Churches of Christ in the U.S.A. Used by permission. All rights reserved.
The Message. Copyright by Eugene H. Peterson, 1993, 1994, 1995. Used by permission of NavPress Publishing Group.
New American Standard Bible, copyright 1960, 1962, 1963, 1968, 1971, 1972, 1973, 1975, 1977, by The Lockman Foundation. All rights reserved.
Contemporary English Version, copyright 1995 by the American Bible Society. All rights reserved.

Printed in the United States of America

The text of this book is set in 13/18 ITC Novarese.
The display type is Bitstream Calligraphic 421.

Library of Congress Cataloging-in-Publication Data

D'Arcy, Paula, 1947-
    Seeking with all my heart : encountering God's presence today / Paula D'Arcy.
        p. cm.
    Includes bibliographical references.
    ISBN 0-8245-2109-9
    1. Meditations. I. Title.
    BV4832.3.D375 2003
    242 – dc21

                                                        2003008938

This printing: 2014

SEEKING WITH ALL MY HEART

Encountering God's Presence Today

Paula D'Arcy

A *Crossroad Carlisle* Book
The Crossroad Publishing Company
New York

For Liz Halpern,
Patricia Prior, and Julie Sibley

Contents

Abbreviations for Bible Translations

CEV   Contemporary English Version

NASB   New American Standard Bible

NIV   New International Version

NRSV   New Revised Standard Version

TM   The Message

The Round Table

For almost the entire decade of the 1990s I had an unwavering commitment on the first Sunday evening of each month to sit at a beautiful, round wooden table in the home of Liz Halpern. At that table, four friends learned to speak aloud the thoughts, feelings, and questions that filled our hearts. In addition to Liz and myself, the circle included Patricia Prior and Julie Sibley. It was Patricia who originally brought all of us together; she knew both Julie and me (socially and professionally), and she had heard Julie speak often of her long friendship with a woman named Liz.

The first time we gathered was supposedly to form a book group. That was Patricia's invitation. But when we met face to face, each one of us confessed that we really needed soul friends more than we wanted to discuss books. This, in spite of the fact that we were all voracious readers. The die was cast that night.

Over the years we did our fair share of crying, laughing, debating, and eating at that table, set in front of a stone fireplace in a warm, upper level of Liz's home. There was a sunroom filled with pots of seedlings and thriving plants to the left of the fireplace, and behind us was a glass door leading to Liz's extraordinary garden of herbs and flowers. Sometimes we walked through the garden, but always we spent time sitting at the table probing our lives for meaning, our hearts for truth.

We couldn't have been more diverse. Liz and Julie were Jewish, and Patricia had explored many traditions beyond the Christian heritage in which she was raised. I was the most deeply entrenched, at that time, in any faith practice and was just beginning a ministry of leading retreats that would ultimately take me all over the country, and then the world.

The ground rules at that table were that honest feelings and thoughts were to be expressed and respected. In the early days, it was a grave exercise in trust. I can still see Liz's face the first time we met, when I spoke about the pain that had split my life in two, and the touch of Christ in that wound. As she said later, this was the kind of story she had learned to distrust with passion! Yet something was drawing all of us together. Could we reach past our very divergent backgrounds, different lifestyles, and distinct paths in order to find a common heart and soul? Only personal authenticity and commitment would take us there, and only great respect would allow space enough for our disagreements and doubts, as well as for points of remarkable convergence.

A verse in Jeremiah promises that God, though seemingly elusive, will be found when "you search for me with all your heart." This collection of reflections and meditations is such a search, a seeking that has taken me through the New and Old Testaments, honored writings, as well as the reaches of my own experience. My search also embraces that table in Liz Halpern's home, where the brave questions of four hearts and the lessons that can be taught only by love were keen teachers.

I haven't studied Scripture in the formal manner that Bible teachers do; I've needed to rely on scholars for that knowledge. But I have held words from Scripture deep within, allowing new meanings and new questions to emerge not only from study, but also from the depths of my life experience. I've learned to listen, and I have become unafraid to explore.

When I first began these writings, a sudden storm of wind and hail, typical of the Texas Hill Country, tore through my small community. When the wind was the strongest, I went to the window to watch the driving rain and noticed that a small sparrow had found a safe, protected harbor on the back of my deck swing. From there he was looking out, watching the unleashing of nature's force. In some sense the writing of these reflections is exactly like that — peering out from a circle of quiet in order to experience the force of words that are intended to drive us toward life.

It's the very dynamic that we four women created at our round table.

As I complete this manuscript, I travel back to Boston to sit again with Liz, Patricia, and Julie. I will read them my dedication and this introduction, which will probably make all of us cry. I moved thousands of miles away from them almost five years ago, but we still keep in touch. The bond we four women created is no longer dependent on being physically present with one another, although we consider it a great gift when that can happen. All of our lives have gone through enormous changes. Together we've experienced heartbreaks and illnesses in the lives of our children, the rending apart of a marriage, the serious illness of a spouse, the aging and deaths of our parents, the birth of grandchildren, the loss of beloved pets, the throes of depression, and a valiant fight by one of us to live with chronic illness and pain. Together we've experienced life.

What does Scripture speak to, if not to life? Doesn't Scripture incubate the words meant to propel us toward new life and changed vision? The incubation is like fire. And new sight is worth braving the flame.

Even Darkness Is My Light

The thief comes only to steal and kill and destroy. I came that they may have life, and have it abundantly.

—John 10:10 NRSV

A thief comes only to rob, kill, and destroy. I came so that everyone would have life, and have it in its fullest. —CEV

My week was reduced to jottings scribbled on a small scrap of paper, condensed notes I'd written during jury deliberations at the close of a five-day federal trial. Most of that week felt like an endless progression of hours, many of them weighted by the tedious presentation of evidence: dates, bank figures, recollections. But these small details had been raised to a level of importance, their interpretation now having the power to affect the course of several lives.

I thought (with amusement) that the selection and swearing in of the jury in some way resembled a carefully orchestrated dance, a minuet. First, the distribution of hundreds of summonses to report to the federal courthouse. Then, our gathering on the appointed morning on the steps of that site. Next, the ushering in of each participant through metal detectors, the careful distribution of jury buttons, and the final selection of three different juries. For the next several days we became a cadenced shuffle, back and forth, between windowless courtroom and jury room. Lunch. Dinner. Home. Returning sleepily to gather again, each dawn, in the courtyard.

When the moment arrived to render a verdict, the import of the long week struck me. I remembered anew that life is a continuing cycle of encounters, none of them insignificant, all of them possessing a certain power. Something large and beautiful can always happen, or everything that *might* be gloriously born may never come to be at all. In that jury room we focused on the actions of one man, charged with a crime. But *his* conduct eventually brought me to consider my own choices, with a heightened awareness of the moments of beauty my own heart might have forestalled.

These moments of life are not a rehearsal for something larger. This is it. This *is* the largeness. And a self-sustaining Passion, distinct from our ongoing circumstances, moves through us and in us, unnoticed, longing to free something within until we finally glimpse all that is possible. Until we taste abundance. Until we know what is real.

In August 2002, I marked the twenty-seventh anniversary of the automobile accident in which my husband and oldest daughter were killed, which has defined so much of my life. The milestone felt significant because I was twenty-seven years old when the heartache occurred. For months I told friends, "I've now lived as many years past that moment as I lived before it." The statistic seemed to herald a final closing of the event, a putting it firmly and fully behind me.

So when my friend Kaye invited me to attend her graduation from a spiritual direction program in Houston, Texas, on that date, I decided to let go of old cautions about driving great distances on August 18. I was committed to not thinking about that day differently than any other. I kept telling myself, "That chapter is closed."

The graduation ceremony was particularly beautiful, and together with Kaye's family and many friends I applauded her accomplishment. I repeatedly thought of how good it was to be there, and I talked with Kaye and others long into the closing reception. I was enjoying the plentiful goodies, the music, and the floral arrangements; only because my drive home would be four hours long did I finally pull away.

Two blocks along I stopped for a red light. Once through that intersection I would drive under the expressway, turn left (west), and be on my way home. When the lights turned green I hesitated for a moment, and then pulled forward. My next sensation was of a driver to my left coming through his red light and smashing into my door. It was an exact repeat of the way we'd been hit twenty-seven years before . . . on the same date . . . at almost the exact same time of day.

In the moments that followed, I felt as if someone had torn away a protective shield. Strong emotions took me over as if the initial grief had just happened; re-experiencing the impact pushed me back in time. It was inconceivable that the same event could repeat itself on the same day. It was too terribly coincidental for words, and it was impossible not to question whether or not there was meaning in this recurrence.

As soon as I heard the screech of brakes and sensed a car actually hitting my driver's door, I became immobilized. A wave of tears doubled me over. The driver of the other car raced to my window and kept shouting, "Are you okay?" He was solicitous, apologetic, and concerned, but I couldn't make myself say the words or take the steps I knew needed to be taken. A thought, "You have to get out of this vehicle and file an accident report," was swimming in my mind, but not the ability to take the action. I kept weeping.

A woman named Pat Kerlin, who was driving by, saved me. She had attended a retreat I'd once given in Houston, and she recognized me. She came to the passenger door and spoke my name. Since she knew my history, I was able to make her understand the significance of being hit on this particular day, at this time. It was Pat who explained everything to the other driver, the police, and even to my insurance agent, whom she called on my behalf. I mutely watched her. Finally she arranged for my car to be towed and led me to the front seat of her own vehicle. After asking me a few questions, she drove me back to the Retreat House where Kaye's graduation had just taken place. The House is run by Cenacle sisters, and after hearing Pat's story, Sister Thressa rushed to bring me inside into the protective circle of the sisters' care.

The sisters sat with me in my bewilderment, giving me tea and toast and providing a haven of safety. I kept asking, How is this possible? But we were all equally mystified.

In the morning, Sister Elizabeth drove me for X rays and medical treatment for my back and neck, which now throbbed with pain. Then Pat returned to help me thread through the paperwork necessary to rent a car for the long drive home.

In one second, I'd moved from a calm and purposeful sense of life to a feeling of fragility and raw fear. The great remove I'd had for years from the emotion of my first accident had been ripped into pieces. I found myself in an indefinable inner space. Because of the years separating me from 1975, I had a long view of that experience, but I was now re-wed to all the feelings and the remembered impact.

For two days I moved in a daze, able to tell only one or two friends about how I was struggling and set back in time. No effort seemed to reinstate solid footing under me. I walked around stunned, in the grip of a frightening vulnerability. The fact that the world can change in a moment was once again immediate reality, not theory.

At first I debated the wisdom of continuing with my scheduled work and travel. It was only because my immediate itinerary already included a plan to spend time with two friends very dear to me that I decided to go on. Both friends were harbors in my storm. I let their love embrace me, and I tried to return to a normal routine. But just as in 1975, my outward appearance hid a very turbulent inner sea. Nothing felt safe or anchored. Around every corner I suspected another shock.

I continued through the motions of my days, then weeks, wondering whether anyone guessed that I was wholly reorganized inside. Was it apparent that my inner world had shifted? That I looked like me, but I wasn't the same? I felt undependable, as if the slightest change or difficulty could crumple me. In time I told more friends what I was experiencing, but none of us were able to find the answers that I was searching for. Eventually I began to convince myself that "why" was perhaps unknowable.

One morning in September, I met with the group of women who are my abiding circle of support. We hadn't been together since the accident, so I told them everything that had occurred. They listened with compassion,

22

with Bea looking at me long and hard. We were all silent until she made a surprising remark. "I think it's about *love*," she said softly.

I looked at her quizzically. She went on, wondering aloud whether anything we've deeply experienced is ever *finished*. Particularly this grief, which had been, since 1975, a continual source of learning and growth for me. It had given birth to new awareness and carried the seeds of a growing openness and trust. It had exposed a light that guided me. And even though that light was inseparable from searing pain, it had prevailed. It had proven to be greater.

"In your resolve to put the hurt behind you and never speak of it again," Bea went on, "maybe there was something precious you were unwittingly dismissing. If you were unwilling to be reacquainted with those days, you might also be walking away from the light within those events — a light that had penetrated your darkness, teaching you the full reach of Love."

And so, on the day most likely to get my full attention, I was, literally, jolted and forced to remember. Forced to remember so I would not forget. So I would not turn away from that which led me still. There it was. The moment Bea spoke, I knew she was right. The crippling fear began to diminish, and a sense of well-being returned. The recently heightened sensitivity to every hurt or sadness started to wane. Now emotions could once again pass through me without owning me; I was no longer in their grip. I'd heard what I needed to hear. I'd been strongly reminded to turn, always, *toward* Love, even if it is revealed by pain.

I began to understand anew that the disguises Love wears will often be puzzling and beyond my understanding. In 1975 I couldn't have predicted that the period of heartache set in motion by my initial accident and great losses would one day reveal life's abundance or would ultimately convince me completely that a human lifetime is creation's greatest gift. Sometimes the house of cards has to fall. Only then, in fact, did *my* eyes open. Only then did I experience the impermanence of everything I was so desperate to secure. Only then did I listen long enough to hear something within me speak. Something that knew me well.

Whatever precipitated my arousal had to have been a brush with Love. What else awakens us? And it was, perhaps, the closest I'll come to ever understanding the breadth of Love and the mystery of being here. Now I realized that this same Love would never cease driving me toward greater knowledge, which is why I must honor it always.

The night after Bea's remarks, I wrote a letter in my journal to the driver of the other car. *I regret entering your life in such a hard way, but I hope that you've found some meaning that cancels out the initial hardness. For me, our accident was a terrible and beautiful reminder that everything belongs, and that I always run the great risk of turning away from the very light that intends to illuminate my path. August 18 is ironically both my heartbreak and my abundance. I accept it now in new measure, and I pray that the same moment has been equally important and revealing for you.*

To myself I wrote: I *struggle, still, to value life enough. To lie, ear to the ground, until I hear, above every competing sound, the beckoning of all that's true. I experience things. But when will I arrive at an awareness deeper than what I initially perceive? When will I recognize in each thing the reality of Spirit, of Love? Then and only then will I taste real abundance and fullness of life. Then, darkness will become light. The truer the recognition, the truer love I will know.*

Surrendering to the Tides of Love

. . . Your Kingdom come, Your will be done, on earth as it is in heaven. — Matthew 6:10 NIV

I lived near the bay as a child, making it possible to explore the shoreline in search of horseshoe crabs and clams without leaving my own neighborhood. But the beach I came to know best was a harbor on the open sea nearly an hour away. My sisters and cousins and I would stick our heads out the window as our car swung up the harbor road, wanting to be the first one to inhale the salty air that heralded our imminent arrival.

We rode waves for long hours, letting glorious swells of brackish water pull our bodies over and over again into the cool, salty sea. At times the undertow was strong, and our mothers insisted that we play on the shore. On those days I loved the sensation of standing in water so shallow that only my ankles were covered, waiting for the sweep of the next wave. When the water flowed back into the sea, all that remained around my feet were magnificent large holes from which sand and seaweed had been indiscriminately loosened to rejoin the larger waters.

The pull of the sea has never left me, and I notice that I can be away for only so long. Then the tides tug from within, and I must find my way back. This winter that inner tide led me to Galveston. I made my way along a beach littered with shells, each bearing small pinholes in their rippled surfaces. Both the pinholes and the pinkish hue of the shells caught my attention. Rare, fan-shaped treasure. I thought briefly of stringing one or two of them on a ribbon or thin rope, understanding in that moment how the Indians were first drawn to such adornment. So simple, wearing the earth's gifts. I stooped to run my fingers over a handful of the shells, but something in me didn't want to disturb the way the water had strewn them so artfully. Instead I kept walking, eventually noticing gull feathers being carried across the beach by a strong wind. The feathers would soon be far from shore, so I gathered a handful for the vase on my table, leaving the shells to adorn the sand.

Shore birds flew in long black ribbons, columns, far out over the water. They skirted the horizon effortlessly, magnificent in their speed and power. As I watched, they seemingly inhaled one breath, changed direction, and then flew with single, undiminished grace in the opposite way.

The birds' motion, their rising and falling, mirrored the rhythm of the sea. It was a perfect compliment to the steady descent of water onto the shore — each wave leaving a blanket of seaweed and plankton littered across the waiting sand — then, its gift given, deliberately and silently drawing itself back into the deep. The water's movement was mesmerizing, the careful way it momentarily knew the land, encased it, and then withdrew.

Is this what it was like at the beginning, I wondered, when Spirit first descended into matter, wave after wave? Was it like a dancer I once saw who took a prayer shawl and wound it around and over herself until she sank beneath it and was no longer visible, having become only the shape of her tender veil? Was creation a similar movement? A sublime dance where Spirit enveloped matter until, beneath its canopy, it created what matter could never create? Until it created life?

Did this great brooding presence then descend in another wave over the newly emerging life, manifesting itself there? Did Spirit hover as it created something, now, that life could never create? Mind? And in that mind, consciousness?

And was there a final tide, a last sweep of utter Love, as Spirit again enveloped life until, from living, intelligent matter, the human soul was born? The human being. The crown of Love's descent. The true image of Spirit.

As I watched, waves continued to move across the beach, combing rivulets and gullies in the wet sand. My toes sank in the cool dampness. I knew there was more. It would never have ended there, with only the creation of an image. There was a guiding purpose, a destiny.

I shaded my eyes to better see the glittering sunlight moving on the water. Is the human being, the true image, charged with lifting this world *back* to God? Is that the plan? Are we charged with manifesting the divine in matter and bringing forth the Spirit that lies embedded in all things? Is *this* our function? Is this "becoming" our purpose, though not yet realized?

If so, then matter is the last stepping-stone of God's will. The final wave. Matter, the first place where Spirit

29

descended, is also the place where Spirit will return to its own Self.

And is that what Jesus meant when he prayed, "Let thy kingdom come, thy will be done on earth . . . ?" Much more than a prayer to learn, were the words his message that we must continue awakening to all we have not yet become?

A Path of Blazing Light

For in Him we live and move and have our being; as even some of your own poets have said, "For we too are his offspring."
— Acts 17:28 RSV

We live and move in him, can't get away from him! — TM

A round, beautifully polished stone sits on my counter, the perfect size to fit in the palm of my hand. The stone's marbled grains of mauve, pale green, and gray would be lovely enough to merit its display. But embossed on the stone's surface is an intricate rendering of the labyrinth at the cathedral in Chartres, France. The stone was a gift to me this summer, a remembrance of my leadership at a meeting in the Tuscan region of Italy that twenty-two men and women from Austria attended. During the course of those days, the labyrinth became an important symbol for all of us.

I have walked labyrinths in the United States, and I know something of their long history and of the beauty of walking through them alone or with others. But in Tuscany I was teaching with an extraordinary team that included Gernot Candolini, a writer, photographer, and labyrinth architect. Gernot's deep, poetic words and his rich experience with labyrinths brought this ancient path to each of us in entirely new ways.

"Just stay on the path," he encouraged us. "You cannot get lost. Stay on the path, and it will take you to the center."

In Italy we built a labyrinth on the floor of a stone chapel. We set paper bags coated with plastic on the floor, using them to define the spirals, and dropped tea lights inside each bag. After carrying flame to the candles, we turned off all other light and began walking purposefully inside those rows of fire. Everyone fell silent, aware that words would take us further away, not closer to the beauty of those lighted circles. For several moments I half-closed my eyes and allowed the flames to blur my vision until I was no longer in Tuscany on a hillside, inside a chapel, and people no longer surrounded me, moving in a careful rhythm among narrow rows of candles. There was only light. And suddenly I was nowhere, and I was everywhere. At the same moment. I simply was. And there was nothing more or less than now. Even when I refocused my eyes, that awareness remained.

A few weeks after returning to America, I talked about that evening with a group of people attending a retreat in Texas. I explained that when we walked the labyrinth that night in Tuscany, after the first person had reached the Center and turned to walk back, we began to pass one another, and in that moment we paused to look briefly into each other's eyes. Some of the eyes I still remember.

To help my Texas audience visualize that experience, I drew a labyrinth onto a large white board. When I turned around to look at the design myself, I realized, for the first time, that the beautiful labyrinth we'd created in Italy was not merely a work of art, but also a representation of something deeply true. The path we each walk, the movement of the soul toward awakening, *is* ablaze with light. We never take a step apart from light. By light we are held and defined.

But on the path itself, day to day, we seldom, if ever, glimpse light. We're more likely to see difficulty, adversity, and sorrow. We often feel alone, not held. There is no sense of a life-sustaining embrace. There is the sense that life is an incomprehensible puzzle, which often goes in a direction we would never have consciously chosen. Far from seeing light, we perceive darkness.

And in perceiving only darkness, so much that could be known is never realized. Looking back, I am sobered by the moments of darkness through which I was unable to see. Sometimes there has been light only in hindsight.

Just before moving from Boston to Texas in 1998, I had such a moment. I'd been invited to speak at a Grief Seminar being held in a small Connecticut town. Since I had a large psychotherapy practice at the time, I was not inclined to take time from my work, especially when my last hours with clients were already limited. I had boxes to pack and a hundred details to oversee. Only a sense that it might be important to go finally persuaded me to say yes.

Following my talk that evening, people came forward to speak more personally. The line snaked out of the room where we were gathered and disappeared down a long corridor. It was over an hour before the end of the line was visible. Then I noticed that the last person in line, a middle-aged woman with shoulder-length gray hair, was dragging metal arm braces in front of her as she inched along. It seemed terrible that she'd been standing for so long, and I hoped she'd take a seat now that she was back inside the room. But she continued to stand and wait for another hour until she was finally in front of me.

My first impression was of the radiance of her lovely, warm presence. She stood there surveying my face with such love that I fleetingly thought she looked like an angel. Finally she spoke. "So," she beamed, "you made it."

The moment felt confusing. She obviously knew me in some important way, yet I had never seen her before in my life. And I had no idea what her question meant. What could I possibly have "made" that she knew about?

I could only assume that she was referring to my long, difficult years of healing following the accident that took my husband's and daughter's lives, the story I'd told that evening. To be polite I said, "Yes, I made it." But I had to add, "I'm so sorry. You've waited so long to speak to me, and you're looking at me with such recognition, but I have no memory of ever having seen you before."

She reached out tenderly and took my hand. "Paula," she said, "twenty-three years ago when your accident occurred, you were brought to the University of Connecticut Medical Center. To me. To my arms. I was your nurse."

We both cried, though my deeper, gut-wrenching tears came later when I was driving alone back to Boston. That evening this remarkable woman told me how she had cared for me and prayed for me. She told me how her arms, during the worst ten days of my life, had tended me. And how she'd felt, at the end, sending me off to navigate the next bend in the labyrinth that was mine to walk. How she had hoped against hope that I would "make it." How she'd prayed that the flicker of light she'd seen in me would not go out.

As I drove along, I was overwhelmed with a realization that those days, for me, had appeared to be totally and utterly dark. And if my life at that time had been depicted as a journey within a labyrinth, I would have insisted that that particular section of the path was unlit. But that night, in a rare moment, I not only got to see that I was mistaken, I got to see the very embodiment of the path's light.

Whether or not we are conscious of it, something holds all of us, and our way is ablaze. We move within the embrace of brilliant light. In fact, without that light, everything would cease to be. What appears to be dark is only the density and error of our perception, not reality, and there are truths we are not seeing.

What if we *did* know that we live and move within a reality that's radiantly lit? That we exist within a greater body?

That the words "In him we live and move and have our being" aren't just words? That the greater soul contains the body and is not merely "in" the body, as traditional thought dictates. Would we walk differently then?

Risking Everything
That Wants to Be Born

I have been crucified with Christ; and it is no longer I who live, but it is Christ who lives in me. And the life I now live in the flesh I live by faith in the Son of God, who loved me, and gave himself for me. —Galatians 2:20 NRSV

The life you see me living is not mine. —TM

"We ask too little of life. We dream too small. We stand at open gateways into the divine...but we forever hesitate, hold back, satisfied with the view through cracks in the wall...."

—John Kirvan, *God Hunger*

These words, copied from the book *God Hunger*, were written on a page of notes lying on the passenger seat of the rental car I was guiding through a deep bend in a road in northeastern New Mexico. The Rocky Mountains were to my left. Ahead was Capulin, the volcano that dominated the small towns and surrounding fields. Every turn revealed a deeper beauty until I finally moved the car to the side of the road and just watched.

From time to time I looked back to the paper and the phrase, "We ask too little of life." A month earlier, life had provoked that same sentiment as two friends and I met with children and young teens in the small European country of Lithuania. During those days together we camped by a river with little protection from hungry mosquitoes and a blistering humidity. But the hardships were soon secondary to the promise of something deep and true beginning to awaken within those young hearts. Their realities were poverty, limited resources, and hope for little more than modest improvements in their living situations. But they'd already made peace with that difficult existence. Now they wanted to learn, to not waste a moment, to find inner gateways to larger places.

"You choose each day whether or not your life will be given over to fear," offered my friend Juan as he spoke to the teenagers one afternoon. We were all up to our knees in river grass, and it was nearly a hundred degrees, but the youth were only paying attention to his words. "Most people live in fear, but there is another reality. There is a force from within, much greater than fear, which waits to make its full presence known. And it is able to change us, if only we'll be changed, if only we'll know that it's there."

His words moved through the tall grass: "If only." If only we wouldn't dream so small. If only we weren't content to take in glory through cracks in the wall. If only we didn't forever hesitate on the brink of our lives. If only we'd fall into God and finally recognize who we are. My friend Richard Rohr, a Franciscan priest and esteemed speaker and writer, insists that we'll never give ourselves over to the greater Spirit, the force within, the force that surrounds us and inhabits us, until we get the "who we are" part right. Until we can say, with Paul, "It is no longer I who live. . . . "

Who *is* the dispensable "I" who no longer lives? The one who stands at cracks in the wall, content with slivers of light and shadows? And who is the one who knows differently?

During one of life's lonely stretches, I remember thinking that my distress could be lifted only if there were arms to hold me and someone to speak words of love to my heart. The desire grew until it became a deep longing.

40

Then one night I stepped back, for some reason, and happened to observe that longing in whose grip I now felt lost. I noticed that it had captured my thoughts and feelings, seducing me. I saw how that longing worked its way into my psyche, gaining access to my being through a belief that I lacked something, a conclusion that fullness was missing and must be found, a feeling that I was not already free. Because of those convictions, a vulnerability had grown, and taken hold.

Yet from somewhere else deep within, I suddenly understood that if I could observe those feelings and that vulnerability, then I was separate from them. I was the one watching. And my watching presence lacked nothing. Something said to me, don't align your thinking with these emotions, nor struggle to become free of them. Instead, become present. Simply observe.

I considered that with one sweep of my observer's hand, an inner hand, I might be able to move fear and longing away. I tried it. And another reality emerged that knew something altogether different than what I'd been feeling. It knew that I was in fact already loved, and already free. Nothing was missing.

"You long for more?" a larger reality seemed to ask. "Then picture it. See it being realized. You have full power to imagine *all* that your life can be, and full power to step into that reality." The words reminded me of the strong desire that had once driven me from a full life in Boston to a new life in the hill country of Texas. Desire alone would not have moved me there. It was *seeing* myself there, from deep within, that finally caused it to happen. Picturing it. First creating the reality of it within an inner realm. I imagined myself there, and then I stepped forward into that reality. The inner reality created the possibility, and the outer reality was attained.

If we were *not* restricted by the ego's limited sight, if we knew within us a *greater* nature, whose sight is truly unlimited, then what would be possible? Perhaps the greatest purpose of a lifetime is to regain this greater sight, to become aware of it, and to know ourselves in a very different way, recognizing every circumstance, both great and small, as nothing more or less than an opportunity to fall into a freedom that is already here.

It's possible that situations are continually offering us opportunities to transcend a limited and ordinary view of human life in order to find a larger life, one in which anything and everything could be born. Living in this awareness, life's events would no longer exercise the same control or power over us. We'd relate to everything in a totally different way, and something new would begin to emerge.

Once, at the conclusion of a three-day retreat held in a women's prison, the inmates were asking final questions and speaking with fierce honesty to one another. One inmate, in prison for life without possibility of parole, asked to address the group. There was a compelling serenity about her. I don't remember her particular words. I know she offered hope and encouragement. As I listened, something far greater than the meaning of her words became visible. It was apparent that she was living within the awareness of something great. Literally. I was watching it.

A light had so obviously transformed her former darkness that the freedom in her being changed the room. The small sense of her — the murderess — was no longer visible. It was completely overshadowed by an inner being who stood at an open gateway. And the power in this being made the portal available to everyone else in the room. "It is no longer I who live."

The power is that commanding. And if we *could* look past what is occurring on the surface, we'd see the utter beauty of the inner nature trying to emerge in each of us. Far from asking too little of life, we would lend our effort to so much more.

Falling into the Hands of God

It is an overwhelming experience to fall into the hands of the living God, to be invaded to the depths of one's being by His presence, to be, without warning, wholly uprooted from all earth-born securities and assurances. And one knows now why Pascal wrote, in the center of his greatest moment, the single word, Fire. — Thomas Kelly, A Testament of Devotion

On a particular August morning, I was overlooking the bay in Oakland, California, remembering that twenty-seven years before (on that date) I had buried my husband and child. My mind drew a picture of those hours. I saw myself sitting alone in a chair by the graveside as they lowered two coffins into the open earth. I remembered watching the two uncles who had carried the box containing my daughter. But I could see nothing more. Presumably the burial was preceded by a service in the church, but I only dimly recalled someone reading a eulogy that I had written.

What I do know is that at that time I came face to face with the human condition and what it means to die before you die. But I did not guess that in that fierce uprooting I was also experiencing the depth and breadth of Love. Love was wearing a disguise so unknown that I had no inner reference point for its force and power. "Fall into the hands of the living God" ceased to be words that day. That day, I fell.

And in that fall I first glimpsed something burning within all that is, driving everything toward one sole purpose: the surrender of our very selves to Love.

Yet the Love that drew me, and toward which I was propelled, was not the familiar romantic love, the love synonymous with my cultural understanding. Nothing in the nature of this Love was an echo of anything I knew or understood, as romance had often been. This Love *was* the greater thing itself, and I was faintly aware that it was working relentlessly to free me from my limits. From deep within, I sensed its power, and knew that if I was ready *this* Love would change my life.

My journal, written almost a year after the burial, included these thoughts: *Always that day will include the people and the sounds of those hours. All the life was gone from me, al-though I could not, as I wanted to, die. Life kept on. . . . And though I could not see it . . . it was true that love was surviving the loss and enduring the pain. . . . Someone, never moving, knew me . . . and did not cease to hold me and care.*

Looking back, with the perspective of many years, it is clear that something within me most assuredly did die on that day, at that cemetery. And I fell. But not, amazingly, into a grave. Instead, a key was tenderly handed to me by a Love I could not fully recognize. Knowledge and sight were to come much later. At the time, with Pascal, I simply knew a single word: fire.

And so it began. My life became kindling. And I encountered Love.

Through the
Eyes of a Child

*Truly I tell you, whoever does not receive the kingdom of God
as a little child will never enter it.* —Mark 10:15 NRSV

I was in McKenzie Bridge, Oregon, leading a gathering of
women. One evening one of the younger participants,
a beautiful young mother, asked me to look over a book
she was rereading for the third time. I read enough pages
to understand why its words were important and supportive to a busy wife and mom. As I put the book down to
record its title and author, it fell open to the following
paragraph:

> *On our way to school last week, [five-year-old] Julianna sat
> in her car seat, looking thoughtfully out of the van window.
> Then she called out my name.*
>
> *"Mama," she said.*
> *"What sweetie?" I asked.*

"The whole world is inside of you."

I looked in the rearview mirror at her smiling face.

"The whole world is inside of you," she repeated. "And inside of me."

When Jesus speaks of the Kingdom of God and admonishes that "whoever does not receive the kingdom as a little child will never enter it," the words imply that you must be like a young child, filled with wonder, openness, and trust. But what if he meant something very different?

What if Jesus was speaking, not of chronological childhood and its characteristics, but of a *state* embodied by children until they pass into adulthood. A state of sight. A state in which *perceiving* things means to know them in direct contact, as a child does, not needing to experience them as symbol or idea. A state where you know yourself to be complete, and you make no discrimination between a clothespin and a diamond. You simply see spirit in all forms, residing in all things.

It's startling to think that our access to the Kingdom might not be through knowledge, but through imagination. Imagination might be the language our life's events seek to unearth. And the way we perceived life as children can speak to us again, and once more we will see the miracle in all things.

What if the child is *the one for whom everything is possible*, and *to be a child* is to know that nothing is separate from God? To be a child is to *see*. It is a state of consciousness that allows us to know the world with the eyes of our true self. To be a child is to be led by an inner awareness. "Mama, the whole world is inside of you."

During my visit in Oregon, each woman spent several hours alone, and many, like myself, chose to hike into the adjacent rain forest. I was captivated by the forest's elegance, continuously watching the few rays of light as they sliced through the high treetops, lighting leaves and ferns. For eight hours, I sat on moss-covered earth within my little circle of forest, adjusting to the greenness. Moss wrapped around the trunks of trees, making a lush carpet on the pathways. Everything dripped with moisture and life. I had the clear realization that everything in that forest was either in a state of birth, maturation, or death. All three, really. Everything that was decomposing was also harboring new life force. From every dying tree trunk or rotting piece of wood, ferns and lichens were growing.

I slept in the forest for a short while, and then watched as wind moved the tops of the highest pines. Lying so far beneath the treetops, it occurred to me that nature is the tangible, outermost rim of a magnificence we barely comprehend. But since we're not yet "children" of God, we don't know how to coexist with something perfect. We work to "tame" nature, dimming its brilliant reflection, sometimes destroying it, often just ignoring it. Bit by bit we dismiss its power, so we can prevail. And we live unaware that nature's balance is crucial, and has great purpose. It is not a backdrop, but another form of what we profess to respect and follow. Our eyes do not yet see nature's soul.

So many things are different if Jesus was speaking about more than an attitude or a state of heart, or even about a dependency; if instead he was speaking about a pure state, a consciousness. In that consciousness, everything is recognized as it truly is. And you understand that the forest you are looking at also exists deep within you. Everything is a mirror. The whole world *is* inside us, just as the child said.

Into the Very Heart of God

Holy Father, guard them as they pursue this life that you conferred as a gift through me, so they can be one heart and mind as we are one heart and mind. —John 17:11 TM

I was leading a weekend retreat and had arrived for the initial meeting of the retreat support team. In this hour, many details for the following days would be decided. I knew the resident retreat staff well, but not the representatives of this particular group of participants. I stuck out my hand to say hello to their leader and was greeted by a warm, resonant voice, mischievous eyes, and a lusty, teasing comment. My mind had barely processed his words when I matched them with my own. Then we all fell into hearty laughter. I had just met Randy Smith, and it was love at first sight.

Randy is difficult to capture with words. Sixty-seven years old when we met, he had a great heart and possessed a nature and spirit that were warmly attractive to the hundreds of persons whose paths crossed his. In a roomful of people, you were drawn to Randy. It was a pretty universal response. Something irresistible was alive in him.

This is our nature, to be drawn toward what is truly alive. In spite of that, human history is a continuing repetition of our stopping short of this fullness, and settling instead for an approximation. Even in the experience of romantic love, when many of the right elements seem to be present (especially the feeling of expansiveness that new love brings), I've often lived in the shadow of what is real, preferring the temporary "rush" of excited feelings to a pursuit of the truer Love that drives them.

But the force *behind* the rush is what matters. It is the soul's longing to know itself, to find itself in life, and in that discovery to be aware of its relationship with all that is. It is an undeniable force. I'm aware that much of the pain I've experienced has come from moments when I've ignored that force, concluding that I'm separate, related to nothing, alienated. Believing that, I've settled for unpromising and impotent connections with others, no matter how temporary, as long as I no longer felt alone.

" . . . So they can be one heart and mind. . . . " What was Jesus really teaching? Was he speaking of a truth that *all* souls will one day recognize, that we have never been apart from God? Thomas Keating says it succinctly: "The chief thing that separates us from God is the thought that we are separated from Him."

How is it possible that the greatest truth, the fact of our union with God, remains unrecognized? How is it possible that the soul knows itself and recognizes itself, is irresistibly drawn to the many expressions of itself, whatever their form, and we remain unaware of this?

When Randy died suddenly two years ago, it was a blow to many hearts. My friend Dave Peterson said it best, "We weren't done with him yet." Not done laughing with him. Creating with him. Being mentored by him. Delighting in him. Not done being in the presence of a large and loving spirit. Not done being drawn to something that was alive within him.

I was in a beach cottage on the Connecticut shore when the call came. I cried hard that night. He had been very much like a father to me. Nothing obstructed the love between us, and it brought great delight to me.

The next morning I packed early to fly home to Texas for the funeral. At 5:00 a.m. I stepped onto the deck outside the cottage and watched the shoreline. White gulls flew in circles overhead. Songbirds picked their way through the beach grass. The sun was slowly rising above the water. A seagull dropped a horseshoe crab from a great height onto the large rock below. In seconds the crab was breakfast for the bird, part of the food chain.

Something inside me started to open, and I saw what I had never seen with such clarity: Everything is perfect and complete, just as it is. Everything is unwavering and true, unshakeable. The crab, now eaten, fed the life force within the bird that might itself perish in the sea and join the power of the water, which would give life to the seaweed. Endless cycles. Nothing dying, only changes in form, while the divine spirit that gives life to the form remains constant.

I knew in that moment that Randy had not "gone" anywhere. Had not "died." He couldn't. He existed in the same way he *always* had. He had shed the form of a physical body, yes. But the spirit that had been alive in him was as present as it had ever been, distinct, but not separate from the spirit of everything else. One spirit, one heart, one mind. The spirit I'd recognized in Randy at our first meeting was no further away than when we had stood together in the same room. In fact, because the recognition was fuller now, because there was nothing to distract me, maybe he was closer to me than before.

"So they can be one heart and mind."

What if Jesus was reaching out to us through his words in order to draw us toward awareness of a greater reality? In order to transform our vision, and our very selves so we can see what we are not seeing? In order to unmask the lie in our belief that we are separate or alone.

What if there is a true identity that we have not yet found? What if we are already wed to all that is true, and it's only left for us to know it?

Abandoning Myself
to This Moment

*Jesus, grilled by the Pharisees on when the kingdom of God
would come, answered, "The kingdom of God doesn't come
by counting the days on the calendar. Nor when someone
says, 'Look here!' or, 'There it is!' And why? Because God's
kingdom is already among you."* —Luke 17:21 TM

My eighty-year-old mother was in cardiac intensive care
at Massachusetts General Hospital in Boston during holy
week, 2002. It was Thursday, the night before her emer-
gency heart bypass surgery. I watched her, connected to
every conceivable machine, tube, and monitor, each reg-
istering alarming readings. I kept passing her a cup of
water to help quench her soaring thirst. The body is
mainly composed of water, I told myself. She's starved
for fluids.

Every bit of the room was colored gray, beige, or brown. Even the Formica on the bedside table was unappealing.

"I'm scared," she said, barely looking at me as I placed the bent straw close to her cracked lips.

It felt like an in-between time, in an in-between place. This was not a room where you ever intend to be. It is where you find yourself. Where life delivers you.

"What are you scared of?"

"Of not waking up."

I looked at her. She seemed so weak, so frail. She had just celebrated her eightieth birthday. Now this drama. Her words of fear moved through the room. I wished the approaching night could speak. I knew my mother was scared about not waking up from the surgery, but something in me heard her words in a different way, with a different meaning. I heard them speak of the possibility of going through the motions in life without ever knowing what it is to be truly alive. Instead of not "waking up," I heard not *living*. Never living fully. Never reaching what you might have reached.

I walked to the window and looked out at the moon. What if we were all mistaken? What if *this* is it; what if this is the heaven of our deep longing? What if it was

Earth all along? What if paradise was right before us, unseen, hidden in the last place we'd look? Hidden in the present.

"You *will* wake up," I ventured to my mother, "on one side of this moment or the other. You'll awaken in a recovery room, having survived the surgery, or you'll die. But I think the challenge is to be *fully* present, to be consciously aware wherever you are."

"I don't know how to do that," she whispered.

"I think that to do that you have to let go of everything but this moment, right now. You have to live it without worrying about the past or clinging to the future. You have to abandon yourself to this night, to this room, and this reality. You can only sink into *now.*"

For the next two hours I listened while my mother reviewed her life, trying to help her feel a sense of completion with what had been. We remembered both joys and regrets, her fondest memories, as well as the fears that had held her back and the risks never taken.

I took a deep breath. "There is a power," I said. "A true power. Nothing exists apart from it. It is invisible, but true. It is the source of your life. Of all life. It holds the world. If you can consciously sink into it, you'll fall into your life.

If you can let yourself move toward this power, then, if tomorrow's your day to die, I don't think you'll suffer. You'll just go. And if tomorrow's your day to live, you'll be inside a stream of healing love that transforms all things."

My mother nodded. For another hour, with soft music playing, I asked her to imagine that she was walking on a beach, and I kept describing that power. By 11:00 p.m. her blood pressure and pulse had dropped to normal. I left her before midnight, asleep like a child.

There is a true power, and it is always there. It is what prompts our search for something greater than ourselves. When this consciousness begins to emerge in us, our most usual response is to *believe* in it. But what if Jesus was speaking of the kingdom, not to inspire belief, but to reveal it as a reality we could *know*?

What if he was saying, you're not listening to what speaks from deep within you. You go only as far as your mind can take you. You have not yet learned to honor your inner knowledge. But this is what you must learn. You must become willing to "know" in a different way.

What if Jesus was trying to elevate his disciples to a level of inner sight? To a knowing that does not mean *believing* in something, but looking *at* something directly. A knowing that *requires a shift in perception*. It doesn't happen after death. It doesn't happen after anything. It doesn't happen only in a place where you go if you did the right things. It can happen here and now. It can happen in a hospital room. It happens when you look at whatever is before you, and instead of filling it with your personal meaning or interpretation, you simply look at it as it is. You accept life, just as it occurs, and let it speak to you.

Whenever believing is replaced with inner sight, something changes. A new realm appears. You have to stop believing, and just look.

Against all odds, my mother flew through her surgery and recovery, outdistancing every heart patient in the unit. When she awakened from the anesthesia, her eyes had a look of wild passion. For my sister Barbara and me, who saw her as she first awakened, it was an unforgettable moment.

Drawn by the Pull of Love

Then all the disciples deserted him and ran away.

—Matthew 26:56 NASB

Just before dinnertime, in the cooler hours of the day, I take a short ride to the high school track in the center of town so I can run. I've been a walker most of my life, and running is new to me. But after repetitive dreams in which I am running with abandon, I decided to buy a good pair of running shoes and give it a try. My friend Roy has been running for a few years, and he writes wonderful reflections about his various races. They often end with a sense of his finding God's presence as he gives himself fully to the contest.

When I took my first run, the closest I came to finding God's presence was when I heard myself gasping, "Oh, my god." That day it was hard to understand why anyone would *choose* to suffer in this way. It's taken time to find the wind-in-my-hair feeling, and a sense of running "with" something as opposed to running "out" of something — specifically, my breath.

Just as puzzling is the account of the disciples running away from Jesus. We read it and know the story. But in our own hearts, I don't think we imagine *ourselves* behaving the same way.

The book *The Star-Gazer* by Zsolt de Harsanyi has been at my bedside for several months. It's a large volume about the life of Galileo, and I dip into it from time to time. Galileo's story fascinates me. What was it like, I wonder, to have been Galileo? To have visualized what others could not yet imagine? To see past conventional thinking. To be right, yet alone? For his correctness, Galileo got to experience poverty, appear before the Inquisition, and endure imprisonment. He got to spend the last years of his life under house arrest. He didn't run, but surely he longed to at times. The unmoving and firm system of cultural conclusions, then as now, is formidable to challenge. No one wants his or her careful universe dismantled.

Is this our secret undoing? Are my coveted conclusions about God the biggest impediment to my next step?

What if I'm innocently misguided in what I hold to be true? What if I'm like the many scientists at the time of Galileo, so very certain of my knowledge, just as *they* were certain that the sun revolved around the earth? What if I'm not seeing my *own* error because I've fallen in love with a story that's familiar and widely held to be true? If the Spirit itself comes, as it must, to awaken me from my slumber, to wrench me from my well-concluded findings into an encounter with something infinitely larger, won't I flee? Don't I feel, as Tom Howard writes in *Christ the Tiger*, that "I began in a cozy way, and [keep] trying to stay cozy, [wanting] things to be safe and warm and tidy?"

Can I handle God rattling me? Is religion a stepping-stone, not a destination? What if the Spirit of truth, the One larger than all human conclusions, came to help me solve some of the riddles I cannot solve on my own? What if that Spirit is trying to help me see the limitations in the story I've embraced? Can I kneel before God without forethought or preconception, and not run away?

I often met the limitations of my own conclusions when I wrestled with grief, and particularly when healing began to occur. At the beginning of my journey, I had concluded (with wide concurrence) that the drunk driver who caused the accident leading to my family's deaths was a symbol of negativity and loss in my life. He was an enemy and a force of ruin. Then I had a brilliant experience during which I encountered the power of forgiveness, and I saw that same man as an agent of love. This new reality defied all logic, as well as every rule about fairness and retribution. It pushed against my boundaries and against anything that had formerly made sense to me. If I were to incorporate this new reality into my awareness, it would demand an inner transformation. It would mean letting go of my former beliefs to expand my sight, allowing me to broaden and move far beyond familiar limits.

The poet Rumi says it well in the opening and closing lines of his poem "An Empty Garlic":

> You miss the garden
> because you want a small fig
> from a random tree."

He concludes:

> Let yourself be silently drawn
> by the stronger pull
> of what you really love.

My friend Janie, who introduced me to these lines, says she has often taken the last lines and broken the words apart to plumb them for meaning: the pull, the stronger pull. Drawn, silently drawn. What you love, what you *really* love. Letting yourself be silently drawn by the strong pull of what you really love is the opposite of running away. But you must decide what you really love and then trust that which draws you. It must have been that way for Galileo. What else would keep you standing still while everyone else runs away?

Letting Pain
Break Me Open

The chief reason for all the misunderstanding [of Christ's teaching] is that it is considered to be a teaching that can be accepted without changing our life.

— Leo Tolstoy, *The Kingdom of God and Peace Essays*

When they told me that my husband and my daughter had died, I was lying flat on my back with wide bands stretched across my abdomen to hold me still; I was bleeding internally, and they wanted to minimize my moving. As I began to cry, tears fell down the sides of my face, spilling onto my neck until they formed a path to the bed sheet.

The doctors could not fix me up and send me off. No stitches or drugs could make this right. Three chaplains of major faiths sat with me. But the look in my eyes reminded them that life has no guarantees.

At discharge, the hospital handed me over to my parents, and an attendant helped settle me into the backseat of my father's blue and white Pontiac. It would be a three-hour drive from Connecticut to my parents' home on the Massachusetts shore, and we stopped in a small town for lunch on the way. I was numb and in a daze when I walked into the restaurant, but as the waitress led us to our table I froze. Directly ahead, a baby sitting in a highchair looked exactly like the daughter I was traveling so many miles to bury. I excused myself and went to the ladies' restroom and sobbed against the wall. Water dripped from a rusted silver faucet, and the floor was strewn with discarded paper towels. Scratched onto the wall was a heart containing the words *Joseph and Theresa, Forever*.

In that moment I realized there would be no miracles. This was my life, and I would have to find my own way.

Several years later I again drove from Connecticut to Massachusetts, this time to deliver a talk sponsored by Hospice. A glass wall separated the meeting room from a large foyer, and throughout my talk I noticed a man standing in the foyer. He was obviously listening, but for some reason he remained outside. When the event ended, he moved into the room where I was gathering my materials and walked toward me.

During my talk I'd entertained many thoughts about who he might be. I'd finally decided that he was a bereaved father, too grief stricken to enter the room. When he approached me with a smile, I was truly surprised. It was a high school boyfriend, someone I hadn't seen in many years. He'd read a newspaper article about my seminar and had come to say hello. We pulled two folding chairs together and caught up on one another's lives. Then he asked, "Is it what you thought? Is life what you thought it would be?" Years ago adulthood had stretched before us like a great mystery. Now we knew what life could hold.

"Were you surprised?" he wanted to know.

I vividly remember the conversation and the question. No, life was *not* what I had expected (hoped) it would be. And that was not the only surprise. Having been raised in a tradition of faith, I'd assumed the beliefs I'd learned would help me weather any adversity. Then great adversity came, and there was a profound gap between belief and the realities of loss. The small story of my life collapsed around me, and no tenets of faith were able to hold me up.

Relentless grief shattered all my borders, and it seemed as if the pain had won. Only in time was I able to unmask the pain and recognize it as a powerful tool (vehicle) in the hands of Love. With painstaking care, heartache began to open something entirely different in my being.

I started to look at life differently, no longer experiencing myself as the center of my own little world. Instead, I watched a force that apparently had always existed, but I had never seen it play its hand before. This force was clearly the center of everything, and there was an intention and purpose to its movement. It was pushing through the events that surrounded me. It was speaking to me.

This force was the power behind pain. It pushed until my pain had served a purpose — to break things open in me. It drove through systems of thought I could never have penetrated on my own. The force ushered me past thought into the presence of Love.

This is why faith is an encounter. And why it necessarily turns things upside down.

When Love moves, it sometimes destroys. B*ut for our sake*. Anything in its path, anything that is *not* Love, anything that is not awakened, will fall away. There are no alternatives. In the face of Love, our lives must change.

The Glare of God

Therefore do not be partakers with them: for you were formerly darkness, but now you are light in the Lord; walk as children of light. —Ephesians 5:8 NASB

Love is often symbolized as light. Just as the star of Bethlehem led shepherds through darkened fields, we write and speak of being guided by the light of God's Spirit. We prefer the light. In daylight, shadows are erased and fear diminishes.

I once lived in a two-family home in metropolitan Boston. One winter was especially snowy; seventeen major storms in a three-month period. Days without sunshine began to affect everyone's mood and outlook. Day after day I rose early to shovel a path for my car, knowing the streets would be icy, parking places few. The most ordinary movements became effortful.

After a particularly heavy snowfall, I was working to unearth my car late one evening. A neighbor was laboring in the adjoining driveway, and when he finished clearing his own path, he kindly helped me clear mine. We worked side by side, our heads bent to protect our eyes from a biting, icy wind. Finally he said, "I notice you often arrive home very late on Sunday evenings."

"Yes," I answered. "I travel on weekends, and frequently arrive in the Boston airport on the last flight."

"Is that difficult?" he wondered.

"It's dark. Sometimes that makes it forbidding."

That same week, I flew across the country to lead a weekend retreat, returning home well after midnight on Sunday. Cold and weary, I turned the car down my street, wondering if the snowplow would once again have pushed snow against the opening to my driveway. Would I have to get out and shovel at this hour? Even with the car heater at full blast, I could feel the night's cold sting. But when I neared my house, I saw that the driveway was clear and open. It was also, inexplicably, lit.

It was March, well past the time of Christmas lights. Yet while I'd been away, the neighbor who'd helped me shovel my snow had restrung his Christmas lights. They covered his roof, his garage, and the yards of fence surrounding his property. That Sunday night he had left hundreds of lights shining to welcome me home. It was late, and I was chilled and bone tired. But in my little corner of the street, it wasn't dark.

Years later that act of love remains a strong memory. It stands out, just as the moment in a retreat when a man who'd been blind since the age of five said to me, "Turn me toward the light. I still remember the glory." Or the incomparable moment when I drove with my friends Susan and Eric down their street in the middle of the night (Susan's only son, Mark, having died hours earlier in an automobile accident), to find neighborhood women and friends from Susan's church standing in their driveway holding candles to light our way.

"Walk as children of light." Maybe the whole effort of a human lifetime can be expressed as learning to see in the dark, to see *through* the dark, to the light. The poet Hafiz writes, "Light will someday split you wide open." And Geoffrey Brown, writing eloquently about grief and the blessing inside sorrow, concludes: "[inside of you] . . . bottomless pools will be discovered. This depth spilling out of you will have a tenderness. . . . If you cut the darkness loose every day . . . surrender it. . . . Finally, the darkness will spill out, and all that will be left will be the light."

There *is* a light, hidden deep within our cells, lending its brightness and power to the small affair we call our life. So much has risen up to block this light. But the light, the luminous God, disguised and unseen, prevails.

In an unceasing gesture of love, this light continuously imparts itself to us in the form of instinct, passion, and love. Walking in light is so much more than finding oneself in the circle of God's aura. Walking in light is to experience that very light emerging within.

Wrestling with the Face of Love

Jesus came down the mountain with the cheers of the crowd still ringing in his ears. Then a leper appeared and went to his knees before Jesus, praying, "Master, if you want to, you can heal my body." —Matthew 8:2 TM

The mountain is steep. People everywhere, crowding, pushing. Everyone wants to be close. A lone man kneels. "You have the power to make me well." The words are a whisper, his throat choked with dust from the road.

He looks directly into the eyes he's been seeking.

"You have the power, if only you wanted to. . . ."

Silence.

A hand finds his shoulder.

"I want to."

The struggle of whether or not to align with this powerful Love is played out over and over again against the backdrop of history. It is our collective story. And although a real power lies within us — and we exist within it and because of it — still we resist knowing it fully.

When that power is present, there are no words. The small story of an individual life, and the greater story of Love, collapse in Love's presence, until there is only Love.

My daughter Beth and I once spent a memorable evening at a Broadway theater attending a brilliant performance of *The Diary of Anne Frank*. The sheer endurance of this Jewish family as they remained hidden from the Nazis in a small attic space above a business in Holland would have been striking enough. But at the end of the play the theater was darkened, and the original hand-written words from Anne Frank's diary were projected all over the ceilings, the walls, the floor. Her words covered the stage and spilled across our arms, our dresses, and our feet. The effect was strong. There we sat, covered by the power of every letter and syllable that had carried the heart cries of a young girl condemned to death. For those few moments, a certain power held us, embracing us all around.

I experienced a different form of the same force a thousand feet beneath the earth when I toured the caverns in Carlsbad, New Mexico. The enormity of the caverns, the exquisite beauty of their crystal formations, the white blocks of gypsum towering above our heads, all created a similar feeling. Eventually the guide led us to the side of a small pool, where he turned off the small walkway reflectors that were our only light. A deeper blackness than I can describe fell upon us. And in that absolute darkness and total silence we heard the sound of a single drop of water. I listened. Solitary drops of water, one by one, had created the stunning wonder of these caves. Thirty miles of wonder.

How would it feel to willingly fall into the hands of this power? How would it feel to say, "You have the power," and wait for a hand on your shoulder?

Do we sense the change that Love's power can bring about? Do we instinctively know that this Love is a *real* power, unlike the many pretenders that vie for our attention? That we will not be the same once it has enveloped us?

I'll always remember a friend describing a moment when he heard some news he didn't want to believe. He instinctively prayed, "God, I'm going to fight this with everything I have." And in the next second, a voice deep within said, "I *am* all you have."

My friend Jim Fleming describes power as two threads that run throughout history and Scripture. The metallic thread glorifies traditional power — defending borders, using armies, waging battles. The delicate thread, the thread of love, causes a shift in consciousness until you see what you didn't perceive before. Jim teaches that during the human journey we reckon with both threads. But the delicate thread is more powerful than the metallic one. It's the work of the delicate thread to open our eyes, moving us toward the moment when we'll wait willingly at the side of the road because we want to be touched by what's passing by.

In the presence of our willingness, Love responds.

You Belong to Me

I am sending you like lambs into a pack of wolves. So be as wise as snakes and as innocent as doves. Watch out for people who will take you to court and have you beaten in their meeting places. Because of me, you will be dragged before rulers and kings to tell them and the Gentiles about your faith. —Matthew 10:16–18 CEV

On retreat in Indiana, I listened to a tape recording of a talk by Henri Nouwen. Nouwen was challenging his audience to claim the "First Love," the love of God, from within. He warned that if you didn't, you would begin asking the human persons in your life to love you as only God can love. When that request is made of others, "They *will* fail."

If you are securely rooted in the First Love, you can receive the "second loves" as gifts. "When you live the First Love in communion with God, you can live in any relationship and not ask from each other what you cannot give. The voice you must hear and keep hearing is God's voice saying, *You belong to me.*" This is the voice of our true identity.

Anna Anderson was a woman whom many believed to be Anastasia, daughter of Tsar Nicholas II, who was shot (with his wife and children) by the Bolsheviks in the Russian Revolution. Anderson's tragic story details her desperate attempt to convince others that she had survived the massacre, escaped, and was indeed the Grand Duchess Anastasia. In the end, although many believed her, she was never restored to her title or fortune. She died in misery, unable to convince the world, "This is who I truly am."

Last summer as I prepared for a month's travel in Europe, rain saturated the ground — ten inches in twenty-four hours. Egle, the Lithuanian student who has lived with me for the past year, drove me to the airport. We watched water rising quickly on the shoulders of the highway as we moved cautiously toward San Antonio. At the city limits, conditions were so critical we decided to leave the road and seek higher ground. Within minutes, a minivan was rocking in water up to its headlights at the intersection where we had just been; we waited in safety until the waters receded.

Several hours later, rain still driving, I sat underneath an overhang outside the airport observing the storm. The noise of rain on the tin roof was deafening. From the corner of my eye, I spied a small bird moving about gingerly. He stopped within a few inches of my feet, took me in, cocked his head, and just looked at me. The bird was clearly nonplussed by the furious storm, if it was, to him, even notable.

Birds always stir me, and when I encounter them in that way, they seem to ask, what are you doing? When will you know where you belong in this universe? I know *my* place, but you still seem confused. Do you yet understand who you are?

It was birds that spoke to me during the painful shock of 9/11. I watched images of horror on my television screen, wondering how so much could be rendered expendable by one moment of terror, and how sense could be made of this moment. Yet outside my window, I saw birds soaring. Steel and glass were shattering into pieces that would not be salvaged, and winged creatures, composed of sinew and feather, were riding the thermals with freedom. When it was reported that all air traffic would be stopped for the next four days, I realized this might be the one time in my life that only birds filled the sky.

How was it that a bird prevailed when steel did not? With what power was the bird so perfectly aligned?

"To be sent out like lambs into a pack of wolves" is a hard teaching. But the world, whose favor we court, *will* ultimately reject us. And it must. On the way to inner truths, anything false must break — false identities, false loyalties, a false refuge. If these do not reject us, how will we ever know to whom we truly belong? How will we know, as the bird does, and hope to live within perfect awareness of that knowing?

When will I be able to say, "This is who I am?" Even Anna Anderson, if she was truly Anastasia, was only espousing a temporary identity, not her fullest truth. There is so much more.

To be truly free in this world, you must learn to see that which exists deep within your own heart.

Only the Eyes
of Love

*We have a journey to make. A long, painful, single-minded
journey. We have to reach a point when we are capable of
loving.* — Carlo Carretto, *Journey without End*

"Falling in love," writes Anthony de Mello, "has nothing
to do with love. It has to do with desire. It has to do with
how you make me feel....What I'm seeing, when I look
at you, is *me*! My wants, my desires. My expectations.
Live up to them and I am swimming in delight. But that's
not love."

After the romance fades, after the stars and bells, a
more mature love may emerge. De Mello goes on, "I
see you are not perfect. You have faults. You are you.
Separate, different from me. Distinct. So I drop the illusion about you and start to get to know who you really
are....I love you (hopefully) through the good days and

the bad. . . . And that's not love either! I've seen through you, but I haven't yet seen through me.

"I don't yet know how addicted I am to having you make me happy. . . . I am giving you that power . . . because I'm conditioned to think that someone or something else is necessary for my deepest happiness. . . . I have expectations about how you *should* be or *should* treat me . . . and that expectation has been part of my love."

It's difficult to acknowledge that within many relationships I've called loving, I was making a hidden demand. It's even more difficult to accept that because of this, I may never have *seen* the one I loved. I only saw my projections. I saw who fit them and who did not. I was looking at my expectations, not at the other person. *Love* is clear-sighted. It is seeing another person as that person is, not as a means to satisfy something in myself. De Mello adds, "Only awareness truly loves."

The unexpected gift of my work in prisons has been occasional moments of unequalled poignancy. Once, following a general evening talk, a woman prisoner asked me to account for God's absence when she was repeatedly violated as a child. "I cried out," she said, "and help never came. Tell me why."

83

There was no simple response. Her eyes brimmed with intensity and challenge. I remember telling her that I couldn't have answers for *her*. But I believed that God would bring greater understanding to her heart if she could open it. I told her that she reminded me of myself following my family's deaths. I never heard anything until my heart softened. It was a necessary step. A hard heart does not hear. Anger renders you deaf.

As she left the room that evening, she brushed close to my ear and said coarsely, "You know that thing you said about softening the heart? I'm going to try."

I began volunteering as a counselor in that prison, and this same woman came to see me several times. The sessions were always the same. Few words would be spoken. We simply sat together. But in that sitting, a sense of caring grew. I learned that she had lost two children in a single accident and had no money to bury them properly. She committed a crime in order to pay for their caskets. She looked through me as she told me that story.

I was painfully aware that we were two souls thrown together by chance in a god-forsaken, rundown room in a federal prison. Even the room's single plant was fighting for life. Without speaking, our hearts knew one another's capacity for pain. The spirit within me looked at her without judgment. I knew that life was hard. Very hard. I knew that pain had long tentacles and that I was looking at a soul for whom pain had exceeded the limit she could bear. I saw her, and there was no longer any choice. In that seeing came Love.

The little room became a place of communion. There was no bread, and wine was forbidden. There was darkness and brokenness, and also immeasurable light. I can't describe all that we glimpsed. I can only say that we were looking from a different place, deep within each of us.

Everything is identified with Love, a Love that flows through everything, filling everything. We just can't see it.

Only from the place of spirit does Love become visible. Everything else is desire.

Secret Places

The lord makes the clouds from far across the earth, and he makes lightning to go with the rain. Then from his secret place he sends out the wind.   —Psalm 135:7 CEV

During a vision quest in 1989, I experienced prayer and calling out for God in an entirely new way. A quest includes facing both the rigors and the gift of fasting, as well as the challenge of spending three days and nights totally alone in the wilderness. Several years later I returned to that terrain where so many windows had opened for me.

Upon arriving, I shivered in the coolness of the morning. Stopping first at the house where I'd spent several nights before and after my quest, something tightened in my chest. So much of me was connected to that space. I'd left to begin my quest with one level of awareness. When I returned, I was no longer the same person. Within that house I had written *Gift of the Red Bird*. In that book I tried to explain the unexplainable. Now I walked around, touching walls and furnishings, grateful to those surroundings for having once been my haven. I moved slowly and deliberately, letting every feeling be felt.

I left by the front gate and made my way thoughtfully to a nearby youth camp. It was there, on the second night of my quest, that I had huddled in a bunkhouse for refuge during a violent storm. Now, years later, I watched the river that runs through that camp, and opened the door to the camp kitchen to read the words of Psalm 135 painted there: God bringeth the Wind out of his Treasuries.

Stopping now at the bunkhouse, I took a grateful breath. I had confronted fear there. There a red bird had changed my sight. I stood still, remembering. Then I went on, hiking to the actual spot where I had lived and slept during my quest. My feet knew the way as well as my eyes did. I had few conscious thoughts. Upon arriving, I took a peach from my pocket and ate in silent communion with the life all around me. I nodded at a tree, half-alive, half-dead, which had taught me many things.

On the walk back to the cottage where I was presently staying, a wild turkey let me approach within ten feet of him. We squared off and sat watching one another. Eventually the turkey spread his wings and flew off, circling the river, leaving me in awe of his beauty and envious of his freedom. At dusk I fed the birds and deer, then walked to the top of a bluff to watch the sun set beyond a canyon wall. The shadows and late light dancing across that wall were pure splendor. A single whippoorwill sang.

This paradise, this earth, is incomparable.

Yet I forget. I often live filled with stress and anxiety. I live apart from the dictates of my nature. I allow myself to live with the limitations my thinking imposes.

I've heard myself accuse the elements of being rageful, destructive, and dangerous, forgetting that the wind has blown with the same fierce freedom upon the earth, bringing life and change to the natural world, long before any of us appeared.

And the sea assailed all the shores with its violent force, shaping continents and bringing life and transformation long before we took ownership of the shorelines, or the bluffs, or the ridges for our own purposes. Long before we built there. Eons ago the earth quaked and exploded with her volcanoes, altering the planet's surface. All of it having nothing to do with us.

No elements are arrayed in dire league against human life. I know this. And if I didn't perceive myself in opposition to the earth's movements, how might I live? What would change? Would I live in wonder, not pain? Would I, like the animals, live obedient to nature's rule, and its perfect balance of destruction and creation? Wouldn't I become unable to persist in a separate rhythm which violates the universal rhythm, the rhythm sustaining all things?

The psalmist says, He *brings the wind out of his treasuries*. He brings the wind out of his riches, his vault, his storehouse. He brings the wind and casts it into creation, waiting, perhaps, for the day when we will perceive our own destiny and live with full enjoyment of what is true. The day when we will know how to exist in our natural milieu without perceiving ourselves in opposition to its movements. The day when we will no longer be out of sync with ourselves, with our kind, and with the world.

The treasuries of Spirit will no longer be hidden then. We will know them by name.

Seeing Past
a Fragile Veil

Where were you when I laid the earth's foundation?"

—Job 38:4 NASB

The thirty-eighth chapter of Job is filled with poetic imagery:

Where were you when I laid the earth's foundation?

Who shut up the sea behind doors, and made the clouds its garments?

Have you journeyed to the springs of the sea or walked in the recesses of the deep?

What is the way to the abode of light?

Have you entered the storehouses of the snow?

Who cuts a channel for the rain and a path for the thunderstorm?

Who?

Who provides food for the raven?

Who endowed the heart with wisdom, and gave
understanding to the mind?

And why are we so unaware of this hand of God, stirring the heavens right in our midst?

I remember the magical, frightening feeling the first time I performed on stage at a local theater. I make my living looking directly into the eyes of my listeners, either as a counselor or as a retreat leader. But when the theater house lights go down and the spotlights are shining directly into your eyes, the stage becomes separate from the audience, and you are alone, enveloped in a separate world. It is as if a thin veil has dropped, cutting you off from awareness of the size and composition of the audience, or from anything else that is happening anywhere else in the world. You have to perform within the shadow of this veil, relying on the energy generated by your own quickening heart. Nothing else is visible.

In many ways the stage is an apt analogy for life. There are storehouses for the snow, and an abode of light. There is a channel for rain, and food for the raven. But within the circle of our personal circumstances, we see none of this at work. There is a veil. A thin, fragile veil separating us from cause. Separating us from knowledge of the truer realms for which we were born.

On a stage, the access point to all that is possible is the single circle of light in which you stand. You give yourself over to that light — to the words, to the meanings, to all you long to convey. And in life, the same is true. We give ourselves over to the intensity of the very moment in which we draw breath. There is no other entry point. There is only now.

The moment in front of me is all there is. When will I stop resisting it? When will I begin to look at life from a different place? When will I search with my soul's eyes for the Truth that fills the universe, just behind the veil?

All the while, the Love filling all creation continues to create in form, take shape in form, continues to love concretely. Love's disguise is so clever that I do not recognize it as a disguise. I persist in thinking that the center of life is my wants, my timetable, my needs, and my plans. When I am disappointed or thwarted in any way, my fist is quickly raised to the heavens.

But I am the center of nothing. That is not the way it is. It is only the way it appears to me. I truly exist in a universe created by and filled with God. I exist because of God, and I exist *in* God. God is the center, the One who *laid the earth's foundation*. It is not a matter of asking God to come and bless my small space, my moment of life; it is a matter of seeing that this life is in the embrace, already, of a great power.

At curtain time, when an actor steps onto the stage, a small, iridescent piece of tape tells her where to place her feet. A circle of light covers the spot where she stands. Beyond that spot are the *vast expanses of earth, the abode of light, and the constellations in their season*. One day, if I am willing to fall into this light, I will begin to exceed the limitations of my present sight and awaken to a totally different reality beyond this present veil. Then I will move toward a truer realm.

Murmurings of Love's Presence

A brother went to see Abba Moses and begged him for a word. And the old man said: Go and sit in your cell, and your cell will teach you everything.

—Gregory Mayers, *Listen to the Desert*

It happens predictably, but I am never prepared. There is always surprise, amazement, really, that the most seemingly insignificant moments will consistently be the moments to teach me everything.

This past weekend my friend Roy was visiting, and he and I attended an Episcopal service. Nothing in particular distinguished this service from any other. There were words from *The Book of Common Prayer*, readings, and songs. There was the scent of candles and light refracted through stained glass. A crisp chill was in the air, foretelling the damp breath of winter. It was an ordinary morning, in the familiar cell of my town, my known community.

At the time of communion, we arose from our pew and moved slowly to kneel at the altar rail, a steady stream of congregants before and behind us. I was aware of the motion of people, like a flow of water, moving forward, kneeling, rising. The rail was open, in the shape of a U, and around its three sides those serving the cup and bread also moved rhythmically. And they murmured. They were not speaking individually or specifically to the people who knelt at the rail, hands lifted to receive the bread. They were intoning a continuous, hushed chant. Fragments of phrases fell onto me. *The body of Christ . . . given . . . preserve thy body and soul . . . everlasting life . . . take and eat . . . blood . . . for thee . . . preserve thy soul . . . everlasting life . . . drink in remembrance . . . be thankful.*

Suddenly the words, spoken in an ordinary way, but spoken softly, continuously, began to lift me and lower me with music and beauty far from my cell and the wooden church rail to inner realms of a tender presence. No individual word, but the cadence of the words, drew me. I let myself move from the reality of polished pews and maroon seat cushions to an inner place.

I had experienced the same glory last summer as I rode by car to visit the Italian city of Assisi for the first time. My every thought was about finally visiting this city that had birthed St. Francis. Suddenly my eye caught a full field of sunflowers. It was magnificent with the sheer radiance of their full bloom. The field stretched, continued. Fifteen minutes, thirty minutes, and still we passed nothing but sunflowers. Nothing but those black centers held by circles of yellow petals, heads bowed. Forty-five minutes, an hour. And only sunflowers, field upon field of sunflowers. I felt them inside me, filling me. They replaced the relentless thoughts that sometimes fill my mind. They replaced everything. The flowers took over and brought me to a place beyond words or thoughts. The flowers pressed gently on the walls of my cell, until the walls within me fell.

Both experiences were in my mind as I began a retreat the evening following the Episcopal communion. I kept visualizing the fields of flowers, the endless rows of yellow, which now merged inside me with the flow of the Episcopal servers, the starched white of their garments and the low murmur of their voices, chanting words of grace. Uninterrupted flowers and uninterrupted words. Streams of both. One voice becoming equal to another. The outpouring of words, like the flowers, had been unbroken; they nourished and fed me.

I began to write phrases in my journal, and I decided to read them while walking around the retreatants who waited expectantly. I walked behind them, between their rows of chairs, in front of them, and beside them, murmuring. *Listen . . . Something's trying to be born in you. . . . The world is only a place through which you pass. . . . Look at it differently. . . . Something else is trying to emerge. . . . Something else is trying to speak . . . "I've come to start a fire" (Luke 12:49). Is your heart yet available to your life? Wrestle with what's real.*

I wanted to shout, *Please* let these words feed your deepest awareness. But I kept my voice low. I continued to move.

Something's trying to emerge. . . . Let yourself be drawn by a different voice. . . . Something's trying to make its presence known. . . . Imagine not being afraid. . . . Imagine not resisting the greater power. . . . Something is moving, pressing through your circumstances. . . . Imagine how you would grow if you listened.

Imagine your mind not in the way, and just for a moment seeing your life, your holy cell.

Rivers in My Desert

Do not remember the former things, or consider the things of old. I am about to do a new thing; now it springs forth, do you not perceive it? I will make a way in the wilderness and rivers in the desert. —Isaiah 43:18–19 NASB

People frequently say, "Paula, thank you for this retreat. I heard the very thing I needed to hear, and it struck me forcibly." Then the individual addressing me will repeat the words they treasured, words I have no memory of speaking. Or a letter arrives thanking me for one of my books, and the letter is filled with gratefulness for a sentiment I don't think I expressed! At least, not in the way the letter writer reports it. As a young speaker and writer, this amused me. Now I find it instructive.

The Spirit is often at work within my own hearing and sight, causing me to hear the very words I need to hear. Or to find meaning in written words that will assist my moving forward, whether or not those words were meant to convey what I gleaned. I do not doubt this. But another dynamic also exists. We view everything we encounter through the limitation of our own paradigms and lenses. We translate new thoughts, words, and experiences (meant to stretch us and move us to larger places) into our familiar body of knowledge. We fit new things into the confirmed ways we already think, making it increasingly unlikely we will see something new. We reformat new information into the patterns that keep us comfortable, and into worldviews and self-views we've already chosen. Eventually everything is realigned with what we have already decided is true. This is all done unconsciously; we're not aware of doing it at all.

A letter I've just reread is an example. When I first read it, I experienced its contents as critical and judgmental. Now, rereading it, I see, in fact, that the letter contains two pages of affirmation and approval, ending with one question, and only one, in which the writer expresses an honest difference of opinion with something I said. Yet the challenging question was all I originally saw. I missed all the language intended to nourish me.

How can a greater knowledge, intended for my own well-being, break through? How will I ever hear what *is*, and not what I've decided to hear?

While I was leading an advent retreat, an idea emerged. I asked everyone to form a single circle. We were almost fifty in number. I turned to face the woman standing to my left and looked directly into her eyes. "I wish you well on your journey," was all I said. Only that. She was to give no response, only to take in my words. As I continued moving to my left, she followed me, repeating those same words to every person. Everyone else followed in turn, until every individual in the circle had given and received the greeting.

Tears flowed. It was moving to look into one another's eyes and simply be wished well. As we continued around the circle, the experience grew in power. It was unnecessary to know one another's story or history. We had our various joys, pains, and difficulties in life. The human experience bound us. In those moments we connected in a new and meaningful way. We weren't looking at each other through a personal lens. Nothing was filtering the giving and receiving of good will. The effect was a distinct feeling of fullness, freedom, quiet joy. Sincere expression was eliciting a true response. Strangers were touching a deep place and satisfying a deep hunger within each other.

We were all seeing clearly, unencumbered by the lens we usually wear. But we didn't know we *hadn't* been fully present ten minutes before. We only realized it as we felt the difference. We all long for this connection. For that brief time we had nothing to protect, nothing to defend. We engaged one another beyond our usual divides and felt what is possible between us.

What will help me maintain this sight? How can I remove the lens that blinds me to larger moments, moments of freedom, and power? How can I move past this obstacle and be directed by the force of Spirit, instead of fear?

While living in Boston, I studied the Old Testament with a gifted rabbi at a weekly class held in his large urban temple. He always kept me on the edge of my seat. The Old Testament stories were familiar to me. But not the Jewish interpretations. In order to really hear him, I learned I had to listen from a place of absolute emptiness. I had to listen while assuming nothing, defending nothing, protecting nothing. I had to listen with trust that God speaks in all tongues and appears in many different guises. The experience changed my perspective significantly.

On the last day of the course (which I had been attending as the only Gentile for a year and a half), the rabbi asked my permission to read some words I had written about forgiveness and the power of Christ. What I remember is not what he read, but how the class listened. The room grew very still as the rabbi read. I could sense their straining to encounter God in a form far from their own tradition.

In that room, I too had learned to listen in new ways. I learned to listen for truth beyond form, just as the rabbi had done.

On the night when the rabbi and I first met, I was giving a public lecture on grief to counselors, therapists, and caretakers. A woman asked me about the role of forgiveness in the healing process, and she asked whether I would speak personally, from my own experience. I told the story of my struggle to forgive the drunk driver who struck my family and the lessons I was forced to learn along the way. I spoke about learning that forgiveness is really a choice, not a feeling. It's a matter of will. I told how important it was when I finally understood that forgiveness doesn't mean condoning someone's actions. Many acts can never be condoned. Forgiveness does, however, require a willingness to love deeply, without conditions or judgments. It means loving until you are able to separate a person from that person's action, leaving judgment of the action to God.

I described the markers that had emerged along my way. First, I made a commitment not to speak of this man unkindly, because words have power. Then I made a commitment not to think of him unkindly, because thoughts also generate power. Ultimately, I learned to pray for him, and finally I learned to let it be. But I never guessed that one day we'd meet.

That moment came seven years following the accident. I described the courtroom where a trial was in progress. (At the time of the accident, my father filed a lawsuit against the State of Connecticut for their failure to provide a required metal safety barrier on the median strip that the driver had flown across at ninety-seven miles per hour.) Early in the trial I had asked the judge's approval to speak privately with the driver when he testified, but the judge denied my request; it was simply not permissible to speak with a witness from the opposing side.

Yet life arranged what the law could not. On the day when the drunk driver was scheduled to testify, I returned alone from the lunch recess and entered the darkened courtroom. I was about to sit at my lawyer's table when I became aware that someone else was there. A man arose from a bench at the back of the room and moved toward me. Intuitively I knew he was the driver, and I could tell he had guessed my identity as well. The moment was charged with the full power not only of that recognition, but also of the destiny that had changed both our lives.

No words were spoken. We stood two feet apart and simply looked at one another.

The lecture room grew quiet as I described what happened next. When I first looked at the driver, it was through my own eyes of righteous judgment. Then I suddenly stopped seeing in that way. A veil lifted, and I looked at this man directly, with nothing separating me from the raw glory of his being. For the first time in my life my sight was unimpeded, my comfortable lens having been stripped away. In that moment I saw the level of love that is possible in life; I saw how we might live. I also felt, viscerally, the cost of such a lens being removed. I felt the ego's wail — then, freedom, just on the other side.

I knew it was the power of Christ (the consciousness of Christ) that drove that moment, responding to my heart's willingness with the *feeling* of forgiveness I hadn't been able to find on my own.

After the lecture, the rabbi had come to speak with me, visibly shaken. He told me who he was and how my story had pushed hard against his own beliefs. Through eyes brimming with emotion he said, "Yet I look into your eyes, and I cannot mistake the truth I find there." Years later he told me that he went home that night, told his wife all that had taken place, and wept.

Once, traveling in New Mexico, I watched clouds building into masses so large and full they seemed to nearly touch the road. A white light emanating from within the clouds was so intensely bright I was forced to shade my eyes. In front of this vista, a single buzzard flew effortlessly, drawing me with him toward the horizon. Through the bird I could feel the thunderous power of the cloud's positive and negative energies.

A second buzzard joined the first, both gliding together in elegant dance. As the birds circled higher and higher, more buzzards joined them from all directions. Feasting on the fire of light within the clouds, I followed the movement of the birds. The clouds separated again and again, creating larger and larger openings in the heavens.

That's what it's like. That's how it feels to let the force of Spirit remove your lens and show you greater things. That's how it feels to see directly. That's what it's like to break through to the paradise just on the other side of the ego's cry.

Glory Dwelling
Deep Within

All of you surely know that you are God's temple and that his Spirit lives in you. — 1 Corinthians 3:16 CEV

One September evening as I loaded my car for the next day's travel, stars filled the heavens with an unusual brilliance. I stopped packing for several minutes and watched. I was reminded of how stars, throughout history, have guided navigators on both land and sea. But they are just one form of light that guides us. Within the heavens of our own bodies, guiding from within, is the Spirit of God.

It's easier not to know this. Less demanding. It's simpler to speak of Spirit apart from myself. Something to be found. Or worshiped. An external force with properties and authority. What am I to do with a union of matter and Spirit? With a guide that's enshrined within?

I once stood in Arkansas beside a monastery kitchen at sunset. The sisters who lived there were at Vesper services, so I stood alone watching the late afternoon light as it moved across the grass. From the corner of my eye I sensed movement. In the sky above, a small flock of black birds began to gather and circle. I tipped back my head to watch. Dozens and dozens of birds began to arrive, more every moment. The circle expanded until I was watching an immense black ring above my head, a sight so magnificent it made my heart pound. The sheer number of birds was thrilling. At least three hundred birds circled that darkening sky for a full twenty-five minutes.

Twice they changed direction, first clockwise, then counterclockwise, attuned to some other knowing. Then they began moving slowly toward the monastery kitchen, and, dozens at a time, they disappeared inside its tall chimney until the sky was empty and the chimney, presumably, was full. Chimney swifts. That's what they must have been. Looking at the brick chimney afterward there was no way to guess that creation had just poured itself within brick and mortar in that way. The chimney appeared to be uninhabited.

The beauty of that sight held an image of the hidden presence of the Divine, of the unseen Truth behind all our lesser truths. God secreted in all things. Spirit inhabiting our substance, feeding and sustaining us. Fire embedded in our cells. All the while, we appear to be only the roles we play, the identities given us by geography and birth. And life appears to be only the events and details that give it form.

Why does it persist, this belief that only the small drama of my life is real? Why don't I live from a greater knowledge? What *is* the temple of God?

What if God's temple is not our physical body, but the luminous, clear, immortal body in which our physical body exists? The same immortal body that sustained Jesus when he walked on the Emmaus road following his crucifixion? The same temple that three of the disciples saw on the Mount of Transfiguration? (*And He was transfigured before them; and His face shone like the sun, and His garments became as white as light.* Matthew 17:2) But they only glimpsed God's temple, unable to sustain the vision. It was a brightness they could not bear.

Does something contain us and at the same time fill us? Is everything immeasurably more than we guess? And in this luminous body, are we, like Spirit, everywhere?

Do you not know that you are a temple of God?

Only Touching His Cloak

Then suddenly a woman who had been suffering from hemorrhages for twelve years came up behind him and touched the fringe of his cloak, for she said to herself, "If I only touch his cloak, I will be made well." —Matthew 9:20–21 NRSV

It was one week before Christmas, and I was sewing name tapes into a sweater for my father, helping, along with my sisters and mother, to send him off to a nursing home as he had once sent me off to camp, many years before. We counted underwear, matched his socks in neat piles.

"Here, try on this new sweater," I said. I'd bought him a navy sweater, even though I'd never seen him wear blue.

"Dad, it looks good. Very good!"

I had to guide his right hand and arm in and out of the sleeve. They no longer moved by volition.

"Maybe your whole life would have been different if you'd worn navy," I quipped. He laughed hard, drool falling to his chest and onto the new garment. I reached for a tissue and wiped his chin, like I would a child. We didn't know that he only had one Christmas left.

I labeled the hamper I'd just purchased for his new closet. My stomach churned in protest of his having to leave this home where he'd lived for forty-six years. But those were my emotions. I was sad for him in a way that he was not sad for himself. He seemed to understand that the rotating teams of health care professionals, plus my mother's continual care and my sisters' constant efforts were no longer enough to give him the kind of attention he required.

I kept working. I wrote his name inside the waistband of his new pants. I'd stood for agonizing minutes in a store, three hours earlier, searching for his size. Then I had wondered if the pants I'd found, with pleats, would be okay. He never liked pleats. Tired and frustrated, I'd finally sat down on the floor beneath the rack of trousers. The plaintive notes of "I'll Be Home for Christmas" filled the men's department. Christmas shoppers were everywhere, shoulder to shoulder; lines were long and tempers short. People had stepped over me, and suddenly I'd laughed until I cried because my father was now tied into a wheelchair and I had finally realized that pleats didn't matter anymore.

I wanted to say to him, "Don't be afraid." I knew he was nervous. I looked at him, sitting at a kitchen table where he would never sit again. But there was no way to stop the moment, or its necessity. The look on his face seemed so vulnerable, so raw.

Perhaps the woman with the hemorrhage was equally raw and desperate when she reached out to touch the hem of Jesus' cloak. Yet even in that anxious state, she moved deliberately and boldly. What made that possible?

Could she see truly? Was her reaching out a true act of consciousness? Unlike so many others who encountered Jesus, did she know that Truth was passing by her? Was she responding in a different manner, rather than relying solely on what her mind showed her?

She appeared to have no need for dogma, or symbols. She needed no miracles to believe in this man. She seemingly had something greater: inner knowledge. She could see what stood before her. And so she reached out.

I wonder, in later centuries, where her simple action would have led if it had been accompanied by these words to us: "Here's where you are, my brothers and sisters, trying to grasp everything with the mind. And here's where you *could* go. I'll show you."

And then she acted, simply and directly. The clean response of spirit to spirit. Her spirit, not her mind, reached out. And in the freedom that drove her act was great power.

I wished such faith for my father.

What Am I Willing to Know?

"Teach me thy ways, O Lord" is, like all prayers, a rash one.
— Annie Dillard, *Holy the Firm*

 Have I ever fully accepted life on *its* terms, living in balance with the laws that govern nature, giving in to those forces and rhythms, rather than struggling against them?

Can I see the crises in my life as anything other than errors or disruptions? Anything other than proof that something is amiss or wrong?

Do I still believe I am entitled to certain privileges and explanations?

Am I secretly waiting for someone else to make me happy?

Am I willing to endure pain in order to grow?

Can I accept the fact that it takes effort to bring about growth?

114

Do I want Truth even if it makes my life uncomfortable?

Have I yet recognized that my points of view are also my judgments?

Do I still project human emotions, feelings, and desires onto God? Do I cling to visions adopted when I was very young? Do I want to see who God really is?

Will I ever give up the illusion of permanence?

Will I continue to insist on certain beliefs, preferring them to direct encounters with the Divine?

What am I *really* willing to know? And at what cost?

Do I have the desire (or courage) to find God in life?

Today I am surprised by some of the questions I've expressed in my journals over the years. But I realize that at the time, I was writing from a different perspective, looking through a lens that restricted how much I could see. Where *is* God, I kept asking? How can I find God?

Once those questions were a matter of survival to me, words asked by an anguished heart. Glimmers of understanding did eventually come, although many of those first, hard-won conclusions seem small to me today. But the early awarenesses were part of a first breaking through of a greater knowledge. And they were the beginning of an intense desire to know more.

I had no idea, not *any* idea, then about the forces bold prayers might set in motion.

I've learned how much of a leap faith really is. I've learned there are secret places to which the mind can never take you. Studying about God isn't enough. Something within must awaken and push you infinitely farther.

On a backpacking trip in Tennessee with my friends Susan and Pam, I remember eyeing a huge tree trunk that had fallen across a fairly substantial creek. I could see no way to cross over the creek to where the trail continued on the other side without traversing the log. I grimaced. The last log I'd crossed over water while hiking had given way beneath me. I was plunged into chilly water and had a very soggy, two-mile walk back to shelter in thirty-degree weather. So I regarded this log with trepidation. Rain was beginning to fall, and I knew the bark would be slippery. I anticipated a freefall; I just prayed it wouldn't be a *soggy* freefall. Gratefully, this log held. It's often like that. When faced with an obstacle, you have to take a deep breath, then leap.

"Teach me thy ways, O Lord." The words have such beauty, but in reality, they are frightening. Will I ever desire and love God purely for the sake of God? Will I grasp the joy of being Spirit in matter? Do I sincerely want to be taught?

If I recognized God — God the Creator, God the Spirit, the One who moves in and out of my life in disguise — would I finally arrive at the other side of this dream that insists that the meaning of my life rests in my circumstances? Would I hear God say, Your life is about so much more than these events you are experiencing? Would God say, Look, the Spirit is the father and mother of all things? Would God say, The Spirit cannot die, the Spirit is the secret cause of being? Would God say, Only because of Spirit is there form?

Maybe God would say: The Spirit is many things at the same time, and that is why there is no single, absolute answer to anything. Listen. At the heart of creation is my delight, and it cannot be defeated. Light cannot be turned into darkness. So don't be afraid. Look from the place of Spirit, and you'll see.

I long to teach you my ways. Will you let me?

The Word Speaking to My Heart

When he entered Capernaum, a centurion came to him, appealing to him and saying, "Lord, my servant is lying at home paralyzed, in terrible distress." And He said to him, "I will come and cure him." The centurion answered, "Lord, I am not worthy to have you come under my roof, but only speak the word, and my servant will be healed."

—Matthew 8:5–8 NRSV

The continuous stress of airport baggage handling wears out pieces of my luggage every three to four months. Last month, before the start of another trip across country, I purchased my latest small roll-on bag. The salesclerk noticed that a lock came with the bag, but after careful searching neither of us could find the key. I grew impatient, but the clerk continued to examine the bag diligently, opening and inspecting every compartment.

Long lines of shoppers were forced to wait until she had satisfied herself that the key was simply missing. Even though this was the only bag of its kind left for sale, she was reluctant to sell it to me without the key. Only my firm assurance that I preferred to use my own, sturdier luggage lock finally convinced her to ring up the sale.

The luggage stayed in the back of my car until I was ready to pack for my trip. So it was just hours before my flight when I realized that because I could not remove the original lock hanging from the suitcase's outer, metal zipper, I could not put on my own lock. Frustrated, I took everything out of the suitcase and searched thoroughly one more time. Nothing. I finally repacked and left, traveling through six airports in the next two days, my bag remaining unlocked, holding my breath that no theft would occur.

After my sixth flight, I arrived in California where I'd be staying for a week. When I got to my room, I took a few things from the top of my bag, and then I happened to glance down at the floor, my eye attracted by something small and shiny. Lying there, inexplicably, was the missing key to the lock. Two weeks and three flights later, a second key to the same lock appeared in the suitcase's clear plastic, zippered compartment, a pouch that had been checked and rechecked, packed and repacked at least a dozen times.

How could so many sets of eyes (mine, the sales-clerk's, my daughter's) have been looking for one thing and failed to see it? Where were those keys hidden? And what caused them to appear when they did? I will never understand it.

So much is hidden from me. Hidden right in front of my nose, and directly in my line of sight. But I will not see it until I am able to look from a different place and am ready to know what I have not yet considered. Everything that contradicts what I was taught and shown in school, church, and home will challenge me. Keys will not be found in obvious places.

When I do finally see what I haven't been able to see before, I will live with a new perspective. And the prior years of pain and uncertainty may one day be seen as part of a progression toward a clarity my mind could never produce. Only the Spirit emerging from within could lead me to this place.

Last year I spoke in a women's shelter in a large city. The accumulated years of pain carried by every woman in that room were palpable. As I began to speak, they sized me up and watched my every movement. Had I not been relating from my own experience of pain, I would have lost them in the first ten minutes.

But we hung in with one another. Toward the end of the evening, they asked questions and told their own stories. Some of the women asked me to repeat certain things I had said. I can't remember two or three hours that were better spent. They wanted to grow and understand more. What they *longed* for was to live in a different way.

Just before the program ended, a woman with a mantle of great sorrow about her asked to speak. She stood. "You have to understand," she pleaded. "This is the first time in my life I've been aware that pain might have a purpose other than to drive me to booze, drugs, and violence. This is the first time I've seen that my cries are not too small to be heard, and perhaps *have* always been heard. I just wouldn't hear the answers. But now I want to."

Afterward, dear friends took me to dinner. But sitting in a busy, noisy restaurant was difficult. My mind and heart were still with those women. I thought, strangely, of Helen Keller. Until she learned the word "water," she didn't understand the world. That was her key. The woman I'd just left had to know "love," really know it, in order to be well within.

I sat at that table, the din of voices and silverware, the noise of conversations, and the ring of laughter covering everything, and wondered what word was waiting for me.

Toward Deeper Communion

Jesus told the people who had faith in him, "If you keep on obeying what I have said, you truly are my disciples. You will know the truth, and the truth will set you free."

—John 8:31–32 CEV

I was a summer exchange student in Innsbruck, Austria, as a college student in the 1960s. Now, thirty years later, I found myself sitting with those memories in Innsbruck's Old Town, having dinner with Gernot, the man who would build labyrinths on our upcoming retreat. I'd just learned that Gernot also led pilgrimages. "Why?" I had asked.

Gernot was thoughtful for a moment. "Because on the road you become a different person. Walking makes the mind free."

The next day I walked through Innsbruck for hours. For a time I followed the river, crossing it by one of many walkways, searching for the home where I had once lived. I allowed myself to become lost in the winding maze of streets, the peaks of the Alps my north star, the river below my compass. I walked through parks where Germans once marched and skirted the courtyards of monasteries. Returning to the center of town, I stopped at a small café and watched afternoon light fall across worn cobblestones and simple shops.

I thought about the potential that always exists in life. Yet, a potential I may never realize unless something else emerges that exceeds my mind and heart, giving expression to the truer mind and soul waiting there. Until this inner world awakens, nothing substantial will change in my life. Only when I respond to the powerful longing in my own soul will I exceed the limitations that human nature poses.

These are the hours of my life, I thought, sitting at a small table in the fresh Austrian air. Across the square men and women lined up at stone cisterns to fill their glass bottles with the pure water flowing from great heights in the mountains. This is it. My life. How I respond, whether or not I am ready to open doors into larger places, will determine what I realize and what my life will be.

Before me I saw the ordinary ways of being in the world, the ordinary ways of relating to life. I saw life experienced primarily as the passing events of our days and the creation of family, community, and nation. Then I saw another way of being and living, where I would relate primarily not to my roles and circumstances, but to a larger self, found within. That inner relationship would give expression to a very different experience of life, and to a great freedom. Responding to this larger self, everything would become possible because I would realize within me the means to exceed fear and to meet any circumstance with a greater power. This relationship would begin to change me.

I also knew, in that moment, that if I was not *willing* to be changed, the reality of a greater freedom and larger self would remain an idea and a theory for me. A religion. A philosophy. And I knew my culture would always elevate my fearful thoughts; it would not aid me in exceeding them.

A year ago I asked various retreat groups to answer the question, "*What holds you back in life?*" Their responses, which all fell into similar categories, were sobering:

The opinions of others
My need to be right
Memories

Just stuff, possessions
Stubbornness
Disappointment that my life didn't move in certain directions
Anger at old hurts
The "good" times, past days of glory
Fear of failure, fear of rejection, fear of not having enough
money
Fear of change, wanting things to always stay the way they
once were

Then I asked, "What *blocks your heart*?" They answered:

Anger
Not forgiving myself for past mistakes
Disappointment in relationships, in marriage
Being unable to get over missed opportunities
Never being satisfied with who I am
Fear of not being good enough.
Fear of true intimacy
Fear of voicing what I feel most deeply
Fear of becoming vulnerable
Fear of loss
Fear of being real

The most moving response simply read, "*I'm so sad. I live with such deep hurt.*"

I kept these lists, reading them over several times. They comprise a compelling picture of what binds us in life. And while no one stands at the beginning of life vowing, "I think I'll bind myself to fear," we still behave as if that were so.

These are the barriers to larger things. This is what fills the hours of my life. And the ideas and attitudes that bind me determine which doors, if any, will open to me. This is the sum of my response to being here. I may be bound to fear, or, deep within, I may find something much truer. If I respond to my soul, in deep communion, everything around me will change.

These are the fleeting hours of my life.

The Unbearable Gift
of Life

*You have your heads in your Bibles constantly because you
think you'll find eternal life there. But you miss the forest
for the trees. These Scriptures are all about me! And here
I am, standing right before you, and you aren't willing to
receive from me the life you say you want.*

—John 5:39–40 TM

To ride in a glider is breathtaking. The cockpit of the
first glider I rode in had a Plexiglas dome, providing
a panoramic view of the clouds and the heavens. A
single cord attaches the "lead" plane, the plane that
gets the glider airborne, to the glider. When the lead
plane's engine is fired and it takes off, the glider begins to lift also. With the cord between the two planes
pulled taut, we rose above the trees, above the birds,
into the clouds. At a signal from the glider pilot, the lead

rope is released, and you realize that nothing holds you aloft save the wind — the thermals. You're left floating in space, listening to the music of the changing currents of air.

The wind carried us for nearly an hour before the glider pilot began skillfully guiding the plane into an easy descent. My legs were wobbly when we deplaned, but not my heart. The experience had been exciting. Strong.

The vantage point offered by the engineless glider was remarkable. From the air, it was apparent that forces we rarely consider actually uphold us. There is freedom. There is power. On the ground, none of this is obvious. On the ground, enmeshed in the details of life, there is little else but the drama of living out my particular story.

How wondrous it would be to pack every limiting belief, every mistaken conclusion into a lead plane and then free myself by the severing of a single cord. How amazing it would be to quickly and swiftly loose the ties that wed me to repetitious acts and small vistas. To become, in life, what I am born to become. To see with clear eyes. But it is not that way. To live in extraordinary ways, to taste the freedom of the soul deep within, to see without obstruction, demands more than wishing. It demands great desire and intense longing. It demands my effort.

Will I consent? Am I willing to receive and have life?

In her book *Word Painting*, Rebecca McClanahan writes: "In 1998 scientists recorded the first sighting of what they termed 'deep light,' a mysterious light that emanated from the ocean floor. The discovery of this light, which was too faint to be perceived by the human eye and could be accessed only through the use of a special camera, seemed to suggest that undersea objects produced their own radiance independent of the sun."

A beautiful description. It was a scientific acknowledgement that the very light that sustains life lies *within*. But it is not only true for undersea objects that lie on the ocean floor. We are sustained in the same manner. It is a choice for us whether or not we'll live out of that knowing, living at the edge of our lives, aware that a light is there, producing radiance from within. We decide whether or not the faint light within is brought to its fullest brilliance. The light is simply there, waiting.

It *is* an unbearable gift, *having life*. So much rests with our own choices.

Moments of Glory

A huge crowd followed him, attracted by the miracles they had seen him do among the sick. —John 6:2 TM

While a student in Austria, I traveled to Venice one weekend with three friends. Taking a train through the Alps, with very little money to spare, we arrived at St. Mark's Square, where we observed the legendary pigeons and wandered through the churches and cathedrals. Great art hung in magnificence all around us.

If my memory serves me correctly, we spent one night in the train station in Venice, not having sufficient funds for a room. Perhaps we had spent that money to ride in a gondola through the narrow, murky canals. We boarded a train back to Innsbruck on Sunday, tired, broke, and satisfied with the success of our escapade. While the slow-moving train made frequent stops at small towns, I amused myself reading the signs in each station.

As we approached Verona, something jogged my memory. I asked my companions why the words "fair Verona" sounded so familiar. We all remembered at once. Of course. *Romeo and Juliet*. And the idea was born that we should leave the train at Verona, since we might never be there again.

I cannot remember being concerned about the availability of later trains, or even checking a schedule. What I do remember is that we walked through fields in no particular direction. With the day darkening, we soon happened upon a stone amphitheater set by itself in the middle of a large meadow. We climbed up and down the stone seats, imagining ways in which this theater might have been used in former times. We'd been exploring for a short while when other figures began to arrive.

All who came, and they were increasing in number, held candles. A kind woman, observing that we four young Americans had no visible light, approached us and gave us each a candle from a small cardboard box. Soon the amphitheater was full, and when everyone had taken a seat, the first candle was lit, and the flame passed from person to person, row to row. We watched this spectacle in silence, having no idea what we'd stumbled upon or what would follow.

From a distance a line of people appeared, all walking slowly toward the center of the amphitheater, each attired in beautiful robes and colorful caftans. Those in front bore musical instruments. And then, underneath the stars and illuminated only by candle, we watched a stunning production of the opera Aida. It was a night, of course, that none of us would ever forget.

It is often that way. Glory is found in an unanticipated moment, in a surprising place. The day seems ordinary, and then something breaks through to your deepest core. The Spirit can neither be predicted nor contained. Miracles are everywhere.

I once led a women's retreat that was attended by over eighty women. As part of the retreat, each woman had been asked to bring something of importance to her that she was now prepared to give away. At the beginning of the retreat, the articles were all placed, anonymously, in a large circle. During the next three or four days, the women walked around the perimeter of the circle several times, admiring various items and deciding which one each would like to "take" from the circle on the last morning. The exchange of gifts, including the telling of stories surrounding them, took a long while. It was moving to hear many "coincidences." Gift after gift seemed to find its way to just the right recipient.

During this exchange, two women, one younger and one older, happened to choose one another's gifts from the circle. Although it was a lovely surprise, and unusual, it didn't account for the tears they shed when they learned they had selected each other's offerings. The gifts didn't appear to have particular significance. In fact, they were very ordinary: a box of note cards and a candle. Neither gift accounted for the level of emotion the two women expressed.

Only when the retreat ended did I learn that those two women were an estranged mother and daughter. Each arrived at the retreat not knowing the other was attending. With grave reluctance, they both decided to stay. Then the exchange of gifts. And a box of notepaper and a candle bridged a great distance.

I once spoke at a large retreat for those in ministry. In my talk I told of a night in my deepest grief when I sat at my kitchen table and imagined myself having a cup of tea with God. Months later, a minister who had attended that conference now was attending a seminar in Boston, where I was living at the time, and he called to invite me to dinner. The conversation in the restaurant was lively, but as we prepared to leave, his face suddenly became the face of a small boy. With great courage he asked whether we could stop at my apartment and "have tea with God."

I searched his eyes. Ordinarily it would be unthinkable to take such a risk with a virtual stranger. But I could find no trace of danger in his countenance. On the contrary, he seemed quite vulnerable.

Trusting an instinct I did not fully understand, I drove with this man in silence back to my apartment. He sat at the table while I boiled water. I slowly prepared the tea, using the teapot and the same two cups I had once used "with God." I was leaving the next morning for a ten-day trip, so I had nothing else on hand to offer him.

We sipped the tea without speaking. I don't remember the silence as being awkward. We were just still. In my mind I was thinking, I *knew* this wouldn't work. You can't force something meaningful to happen. Nevertheless, a penetrating sadness was beginning to grip me. I kept glancing at his face. I had no idea, really, who he was or what pain he lived with. I just felt that something deep within him longed to touch something true. And whatever he sought had obviously eluded him. I sat there praying for him to one day find what he was looking for.

Then without thinking, in a daze, I dimly remembered that I had bought a loaf of bread that day, and it was in my briefcase. The purchase had made no sense at all, even at the time. I lived alone and I was leaving for ten days. No one buys a loaf of homemade bread on the eve of a trip. Nevertheless, I remembered that the bread was there, and without giving it much thought, I went to the kitchen, took it from my briefcase and cut a large slice. Still without words, I put the bread in front of the minister. Cookies or a slice of pie would have been more appropriate, I knew that. But the bread was all I had.

He looked at the plate for several moments, then took the bread and broke it into two pieces, handing half to me. I put it to my mouth not thinking anything. It was just a slice of bread. But the minute that bread touched both of our lips, he sobbed out loud. Tears filled the minister's eyes. We were both hit hard by a force that was palpable. We never finished the tea or the bread. When he composed himself, he moved toward the door and I drove him back to his hotel in silence. I couldn't have spoken if I'd needed to.

God may have responded to my prayer that night, but I doubt it. I don't think that's what God responds to. I think God responded to *the love in the prayer.* I think God responded because both hearts were open.

Everything, really, is miracle. Verona, on starlit nights. A simple box of note cards and an ordinary candle. A pot of tea. A slice of bread. If only we could always see the real wonder of things.

The crowds surrounding Jesus kept asking him to produce miracles in order to sustain their belief. Give us signs, give us wonders! All the while, something great had already consciously taken on limitation in order to give rise to something even greater.

Wherever there is love, there will be the emergence of this power. The question is, will we see it? And will we allow ourselves to be changed?

It Was You All Along

When I consider your heavens, the work of your fingers, the moon and the stars, which you have set in place, what is man that you are mindful of him, the son of man that you care for him?   —Psalm 8:3–4 NIV

We all begin in the same place, a place of mystery. Every person you'll ever meet is reflecting back a part of that mystery. Usually we must be broken open in order to see it. Until then, we see events and causes. We see the small story. We see only what's happening on the outermost level.

Frederick Buechner says, "Listen to your life. See it for the fathomless mystery that it is...touch, taste, smell your way to the holy and hidden heart of it because in the last analysis *all* moments are key moments, and life itself is grace."

Few moments are as remarkable to witness as when someone who has listened hard to life suddenly encounters a portion of the "fathomless mystery" they have never glimpsed before. I encountered such a listener in a Massachusetts prison. During her long years in prison, she had reviewed not only her past and the mistakes that led to her imprisonment, but also the day-to-day, seemingly inconsequential hours spent in confinement. I urged her to write about these "ordinary" events, and a power began to emerge from her stories. In the telling it became obvious that the relationships between many of the women in prison were characterized by an unusual love. A caring far beyond the usual definition. A giving from their poverty that was imbued with a certain tender compassion.

One particular story told of an occasion when a woman's mother was dying. She was given the option of visiting her mother for fifteen minutes while she was still alive, or viewing her for fifteen minutes after she was dead. Either choice would require her to wear shackles, handcuffs, and a waist chain and be in the company of her bodyguards. Given those conditions, the mother herself decided that she couldn't bear the thought of seeing her only daughter for the last time in that way.

stead, a kind member of the prison staff arranged to take a photo of the inmate to send to her mother. Fellow prisoners contributed their widow's mite to help her look presentable — hair spray, shampoo, makeup — all items that were dear and could not easily be replenished. An ordinary act elevated everyone who participated, but they could not fully describe what had happened. They only knew that for a brief time, in spite of the reality of guards and locks and iron bars, they were free. In the unselfishness of their love, something had touched them.

C. S. Lewis is believed to have said of God, "So it was you all along."

So, it was you all along.

It was *your* exquisite timing.

It was you in every human contact, every event.

You, asking whether I will tolerate longing in order to change.

You, standing beside me on the highway when the drunk driver hit our car.

It was you asking whether I will endure loss and heartache when it's my turn to do so.

You, asking whether I am willing to grow.

You, waiting for me to see the mystery in every human face, in every moment.

You, disguised as anyone I ever loved.

You, disguised as anyone who ever caused me pain.

You, holding me when I buried my family.

You, when my small images of you broke into a million pieces, saying, *Let the images break! Let them go! I am not an image. I am.*

You, saying I will pursue you every hour until you remember who you are.

You, saying I have never moved.

You, saying let me get close enough to open your inner eyes.

You, in a women's prison, exchanging grace for lipstick, hairspray, and a roll of film.

You, saying I will love you until you love.

All along, it was you.

The Force of Love

We don't yet see things clearly. We're squinting in a fog, peering through a mist. But if won't be long before the weather clears and the sun shines bright! We'll see it all then, see it all as clearly as God sees us, knowing him directly just as he knows us! — 1 Corinthians 13:12–13 TM

In *Daughter of Jerusalem*, Thom Lemmons writes: "[Jesus' words] become part of us. But some people don't like that. They want to keep the words outside. They want to handle them the way they handle a cup or knife. They want to decide about them, think of ways to use them. But his words aren't like that. His words can't be used. They can't be handled. His words can't be judged. *They judge us.*"

When I first saw the film, *Schindler's List*, its impact on me was forceful. In the last thirty minutes of the film, the full power of the story came to me. I looked anew, along with Schindler, at the true nature of love. For all he'd

142

done, the hundreds of lives he'd saved, he also saw that he had failed to love with complete abandon. He saw that he could have loved more. With him, I considered the stinginess of my own loving. I saw the judgments I've harbored, the times of feeling "better than" someone else. I remembered situations when hurt or fear had persuaded me to cut off love. If I *could* cut it off, was it really love?

In the gospels Jesus speaks of the possibilities of a greater love here on earth. But we don't dream of such love here, in this world. Not really. We don't believe it is possible here and now. We resist realizing that the Spirit can exist when and where we are. We insist that it will only be realized elsewhere, at another time. Secure with that belief, we excuse ourselves from greater efforts. We learn to be good and to treat well those who treat us well. But we don't give ourselves over to that which demands not goodness, but greatness.

And the secret inner nature remains hidden. We do not become a force for love.

Chiune Sugihara was a Japanese consul in Kaunas, Lithuania, in 1940. Lithuanians came to revere him for his gentleness and his command of Russian, which gave them a language in common. When the Soviets entered the city that year, Jews stormed the embassy to secure exit visas in order to flee. Nazi troops were expected to reach Lithuania quickly, and the Soviets wanted Sugihara out within three weeks.

Sugihara cabled Tokyo for permission to grant visas for the desperate Jews. When permission was denied, Sugihara tore up the cable and began to sign exit visas anyway. The story is told that he worked twenty hours a day, "pausing only for tea and for [his wife] to massage his hand, circulate his blood. He was still signing the morning he left. . . . He rolled down the window of his car and signed [another] visa. Later in the hotel, the door banged all night. He sat at a rented desk, stamping the passports with a smile, and a bow.

"On the train platform, more were waiting, so he used luggage, books and people's backs as hard surfaces. He was still signing as the train began to pull away. He had to hand the last one back through the moving window. . . .

"Years later, an American rabbi asked him why he did it. He thought for a moment, then replied: 'I don't understand the question.' "

One day we'll *know him directly just as he knows us.* For now, we *peer through a mist.*

Seeking with All My Heart

You will seek me and find me when you seek me with all your heart. —Jeremiah 29:13 NIV

In the months immediately following the completion of these pages, I'm scheduled to take a short respite from several years of continuous travel. The space ahead looks inviting, but it also triggers introspection. Where have I been? Has it mattered? Which encounters, if any, have affected any of our lives?

I have spoken at countless retreats, meeting many other travelers. Most persons attending a retreat would say they are searching for something, and they may articulate their desire. But how great is the chasm between the goals we voice and actually seeking with all our heart? In the presence of a very passionate heart, I am always aware of how far I still have to go. It's relatively effortless to be attentive to life, to listen, to utilize the talents and gifts we are given. But what does it mean to put my life where I say my heart is and to seek no matter where the spirit leads me?

Seeking with all one's heart conjures images of far-flung lands and sacred mountaintops. But I know it isn't that. It is an intention, not a pilgrimage. It is a wanting.

Almost a year ago I asked a friend why he was risking so much in his life (job security and the approval of others) in order to strike out on an entirely new path. His words still haunt me. "I long for this," he whispered. "My soul longs."

I'm aware of the things for which my ego longs. But what about my soul?

Will I understand one day that there is no "protection"? There is God. And all the circumstances of my life are only pointing *toward* something. Toward the greatest thing. What matters is not the circumstances, but what's speaking through them, pushing through them, pushing through me, moving me toward a different birth.

I have to decide for myself, will I, or will I not, let this Love show me what is possible?

Will I stop focusing forever on what was *not* given to me and stop regretting the gifts that were brief? Will I see the beauty right before me? Will I risk my heart and fully experience being here? Will I say yes to the life I am being offered?

If I allow all the things that once defined me to change, will a knowledge emerge from deep within, teaching me that the final say is not the appearance of things? That the human being is evolving, still, and there are many truths left to discover?

Will I one day grow weary of breaking up my life into little pieces, always responding out of fear? Instead, will I meet fear with something from within that is greater? Will I begin moving toward that which awaits and not look back?

Before I die, will I seek with all my heart?

Beneath the Roaring Ocean

In the beginning God created the heavens and the earth. The earth was barren, with no form of life; it was under a roaring ocean covered with darkness. But the Spirit of God was moving over the water." —Genesis 1:1–2 CEV

My maternal grandmother made braided rugs. Beautiful, large oval rugs in warm, rich colors that she and my mother both used to decorate their hardwood floors. Watching my grandmother work was fascinating. She began with long strips of soft wool, keeping her colors separate and the tension on the braids strong by using clothespins to hold everything in place. When it was time to sew the braids together, she used a needle larger than any I had ever seen.

Although braiding wool for rugs may not be considered a form of weaving, I thought it was. Through the eyes of a child, joining these long strands of fabric to-gether to form a new creation, the rug, was dazzling. And my grandmother was equally skillful in the kitchen. She was magically clever with flour, eggs, and butter. I stood at her elbow to learn how to knead dough with just the right flourish. We all considered her baking to be unparalleled in excellence. Perhaps she sometimes used a cake mix from a box, but not when I was present. Everything was fresh, and everything was from scratch. She emptied ingredients from her pantry shelf and spice rack with alarming speed, but it always resulted in a confection of sheer delight.

This mastery of my grandmother's, enabling her to take scraps of things or various ingredients and work with them until she had a new creation is a strong image I carry with me. She embodied the creative process for me. I didn't know, then, that to *participate* in this process, this creation of life, is what life *demands*.

Can anything be less respectful of life than to wait for a better time and place, knowing we have been handed the incomparable gift of the day we are living? That we are embraced, moment by moment, by the very Love that first troubled the waters? Sent forth by that Love to continue evolving and creating until we awaken to the nature within us already.

If only a voice could whisper to us each morning, *Pay attention. You're looking at something incredibly beautiful. It's called NOW. Just for a moment, listen to it. Take it in.*

There's enough love. There's healing, if you want to be well. There's joy, if you won't put conditions on how it appears, if you'll let it come in a thousand different ways.

Watch the natural world. Feel the wind.

DON'T BE AFRAID.

You have never walked alone. You are not alone. There is within you that which is greater than anything you will ever face. It is the greatest power in creation. Take a deep breath.

You will take your suffering consciously or unconsciously. If you take it consciously, everything will begin to open.

The greater soul is real, and every creature utters the divine mystery.

It is humankind that has said God is apart from creation. God is not removed. God is near.

If you could let go of your names for God, and your ideas about God, and your good works to please God, there would be nothing left to encounter but God.

The true, original creation puts out forms of itself in order to exist in the world as a person, separate and distinct. This is in you and in everyone, either in full bloom or in potentiality.

Let the eyes of your inner being begin to focus.

You, like the biblical figures, are wrestling with the face of Love. Your true character, the God-given character, is trying to emerge.

Everything you know and are and experience and touch is Spirit giving itself, the Soul giving itself, consenting, in sacrifice, to nourish its human part into awareness. Giving, giving, giving to you and to all lesser forms so you will evolve.

So walk, now, as a child of light. Use your time. This is your life. This is it.

The Round Table Revisited

In December 2002, I did make my planned visit to Liz's home. Patricia and Julie were there, waiting. We told one another stories about the experiences we'd had since our last meeting. It was easy to bare our souls in that circle of great caring and love.

At some point during the evening we got up to stretch and pour ourselves more tea and coffee. I was the first to return to the table, and I briefly found myself sitting there alone. Suddenly, and just for a moment, a dense veil which normally obscures my vision was pulled back. In that instant I stood free, no longer identifying myself with my name, my seat at that table, or my life's story. I became an observing witness to that person I know as myself, as well as to all our stories, and to the span of life itself. I stepped outside of my usual consciousness. In that space, the temporary nature of a human lifetime became very apparent. From this vantage point I was acutely aware that within a lifespan we either lend ourselves to the emergence of something extraordinary, or we repeat an endless stream of choices based on fear. With each day, wonder and delight labor to be born. The question remained, would I yield to them?

The Indian writer Aurobindo says, "In darkness' core [Truth] digs out wells of light." The words are my reminder that it only remains for me to seek with everything that I am, letting the wells of light illuminate my path.

The memory of perceiving from that different consciousness is still clear, but the actual experience passed quickly. It was a moment — a moment when a secret sense seemed to awaken in me. A larger thought revealed something to my silent soul. Then it passed, and I was once again looking out with my familiar vision. Liz and Julie and Patricia returned to the table with cups of tea and coffee, and we continued our conversation. We stayed later than any of us had intended, and Julie and I ended up spending the night in Liz's guestrooms. Dawn came quickly bringing a new day, whatever I would make of it, and whatever I would meet it with. It was up to me. What did I really want?

Notes

Page 38: Quotation from John Kirvan, *God Hunger* (Notre Dame, Ind.: Sorin Books, 1999), 162.

Page 44: Quotation from Thomas Kelly, *A Testament of Devotion* (New York: Harper & Row, 1941), 56.

Page 45: Quotation from Paula D'Arcy, *Song for Sarah* (Wheaton, Ill.: Harold Shaw Publishers, 1979), 111–12.

Page 47: Quotation from Denise Roy, *My Monastery Is a Minivan* (Chicago: Loyola Press, 2001), 201.

Page 53: "The chief thing that separates us ..." Thomas Keating, *Open Mind, Open Heart* (New York: Continuum, 1997), 44.

Page 63: "I began in a cozy way ..." Thomas Howard, *Christ the Tiger* (San Francisco: Ignatius Press, 1990), 19.

Page 64: "You miss the garden ..." from *The Illuminated Rumi* by Coleman Barks Michael Green, copyright © 1997 by Coleman Barks and Michael Green. Used by permission of Broadway Books, a division of Random House, Inc.

Page 66: Quotation from Leo Tolstoy, *The Kingdom of God and Peace Essays* (London: Oxford University Press, 1942), 130.

Page 72: "Light will someday ..." Hafiz, from Daniel Ladinsky, *The Subject Tonight Is Love* (Myrtle Beach, S.C.: Pumpkin House Press,

1996), 43; copyright © 1996, 2003 by Daniel Ladinsky. Reprinted by permission of the author.

Page 72: Quotation from Geoffrey Brown, "The Blessing Inside Sorrow." This poem was handed to the author by a retreatant in the 1990s. No attempts to learn whether or not it is a published work, in order to credit the poet, have proved fruitful.

Page 74: Author's personal paraphrase of Matthew 8:1–4, inspired by the words of eminent Bible scholar Dale Bruner, when they were leading a retreat based on Matthew's Gospel in 2001.

Page 78: Quotation from Henri Nouwen, *The Inner Voice of Love* (New York: Doubleday, 1996), 70–71.

Page 78: Quotation from Jurgen Beumer, *Henri Nouwen* (New York: Crossroad, 1997), 104–9.

Page 82: Quotation from Carlo Carretto, *Journey without End* (Notre Dame, Ind.: Ave Maria Press, 1985), 37.

Page 82: "Falling in love . . ." Anthony de Mello, *Awareness* (New York: Doubleday, 1990), 118.

Page 86: Paula D'Arcy, *Gift of the Red Bird* (New York: Crossroad, 1996).

Page 94: Quotation from Gregory Mayers, *Listen to the Desert* (Liguori, Mo.: Triumph Books, 1996), 1.

Page 94: Quotation from Rite One, *The Book of Common Prayer* (New York: Church Publishing Incorporated, 1979), 338.

Page 114: Quotation from Annie Dillard, *Holy the Firm* (New York: Harper & Row, 1977), 19.

Page 130: "In 1998 scientists recorded..." Rebecca McClanahan, *Word Painting* (Cincinnati: Writers Digest Books, 1994), 22.

Page 138: "Listen to your life..." Frederick Buechner, *Listening to Your Life* (San Francisco: HarperSanFrancisco, 1992), 1.

Page 142: "[Jesus' words] become part..." Thom Lemmons, *Daughter of Jerusalem* (Sisters, Ore.: Multnomah, 1999), 261–62.

Page 142: *Schindler's List* (Universal City, Calif.: Universal City Studios, Inc., 1993). Oskar Schindler, a member of the Nazi party, saved the lives of more than eleven hundred Jews during the Holocaust.

Page 144: Quotations from Devin Stuart Brodie, "I Would Not Disobey God." *Sojourners Magazine* (November/December 2002): 9.

Page 153: Quotation from Sri Aurobindo, *Savitri* (Pondicherry, India: Sri Aurobindo Ashram, Publication Department, 1950–51), 41.

Acknowledgments

My heartfelt thanks to the Crossroad team — Gwendolin Herder, Christine Phillips, Jim Phillips, John Jones, Maria Devitt, Matthew Laughlin, and Jackie Andre, They make it all possible, they make everything work, they are always available and I appreciate them and the standards of excellence they uphold. And also thanks to John Eagleson of ediType who has worked with Crossroad Carlisle Books to artfully and beautifully design and typeset this book.

Special thanks to Shirley Coe for her extraordinary copyediting and proofreading.

For my editor, Roy M. Carlisle, I have no adequate words. He makes writing books an experience anyone would want. Knowing that his eye, his pen, and his heart will pass over my words is deeply reassuring and grounding. His deep, intuitive guidance is without equal; he is a born editor. Roy's support and care for us, his authors, absolutely draws the best from each of us. He nurtures and challenges, all in the same breath. Then, just when you think you've gotten as far as you can go, he leans in and says, "Reach higher."

Grateful love to my daughter, Beth. Because of our conversations, which grow richer with the passing years, I write from a deeper place, and I am increasingly able to look at life without my "usual" lens. In every good way, Beth stretches me and teaches me about the real meaning of love.

With deepest gratitude to Egle Pilipaviciute, who has lived with me this past year, far from her native Lithuania, in order to earn a college degree. She masterfully learned the rigors of living with a writer who's writing and, therefore, cannot be disturbed for long stretches. During the days of final deadlines, she prepared my meals, ran errands, kept the house quiet, and never once complained. I could not have asked for anyone to be more respectful and supportive.

With sincere appreciation to my sisters Barbara, Beverly, and Anne, and to my mother, Barbara, for letting me tell stories from our lives. I live a great distance away from all of them, and in spite of the fact that my sisters are each accomplished in their chosen professions and have demanding lives, they interrupt whatever they're doing when I arrive to visit, making time and space to be family. I am proud of each of them for what they create and give to this world.

Thanks to Kim and Margaret Wheless for bringing me to the Port of Galveston, Texas, and gifting me with several wonderful days of solitude for writing in a beautiful condo on the beach.

Thanks to Mary and Chip Cox for an unequalled writing week at their home on the bay in Texas. No words will ever express my love and gratitude.

Thanks to Bude and Pam Van Dyke for being resources about Episcopal services and *The Book of Common Prayer*, but mostly for being such dear friends.

Thanks to these friends for letting me tell our stories and for filling my life with such richness: Kaye Bernard, Janie Cook, Susan and Eric Goldby, Juan Robledo, Jim Fleming, Gernot Candolini, Bea Brock, Pat Kerlin, and David Peterson.

Thanks to Madeline Tyng for taking my photograph for the book jacket, and to Susan Oakley, Mary Cox, and Kirby Hlavaty for their great assistance! Their friendship is pure joy.

158

And special gratitude to Peter Navarra, who has immeasurably brightened my life. Seeing life through his young eyes is a constant gift. He is bright, creative, and so filled with potential. Being with Peter is one of the best things I do.

About the Author

Paula D'Arcy, a writer, retreat leader, and conference and seminar speaker, travels widely in the United States, Canada, and abroad. She is also President of the Red Bird Foundation, which supports the growth and spiritual development of those in need and furthers a ministry both to those in prison and those living in third world or disadvantaged cultures.

A psychotherapist who has ministered to those facing issues of grief and loss, Paula worked with the Peale Foundation, founded by Dr. Norman Vincent Peale, from 1980 until his death in 1993. In recent years she has frequently teamed with Richard Rohr in presenting seminars on the Male/Female Journey. Her individual work includes leading women in Initiation and Rites of Passage.

Paula's ministry grew from personal tragedy. In 1975 she survived a drunk driving accident which took the lives of her husband and twenty-one-month-old daughter. Pregnant at the time, Paula survived the accident to give birth to a second daughter, Beth Starr, who currently pursues a career as a professional actress.

For more information, including a speaking itinerary, visit *www.redbirdfoundation.com*.